Centre for Sri Aurobindo Studies Publication

Classical Indian Philosophy Reinterpreted

Centre for Sri Aurobindo Studies Publication

Classical Indian Philosophy Reinterpreted

by
Victoria Lysenko
Michel Hulin

Decent Books
New Delhi

in collaboration with
Jadavpur University, Kolkata

Cataloging in Publication Data — DK
[Courtesy: D.K. Agencies (P) Ltd. <docinfo@dkagencies.com>]

Lysenko, Victoria, 1953-
Classical Indian philosophy reinterpreted / by Victoria Lysenko, Michel Hulin.
vii, 155 p.; 23 cm.
Includes bibliographical references.
Includes index.
ISBN 8186921362

1. Philosophy, Hindu. 2. Philosophy, Indic.
I. Hulin, Michel, 1936- II. Title.

DDC 181.4 22

ISBN 81-86921-36-2
First Published in India in 2007

Published by:
Decent Books
D-36/A-1, Mohan Garden
Najafgarh Road
New Delhi - 110 059
Ph. (011) 2535-3435

in collaboration with
Jadavpur University
Kolkata (West Bengal)

Distributed by:
D.K. Printworld (P) Ltd.
Regd. office : *'Sri Kunj,'* F-52, Bali Nagar
Ramesh Nagar Metro Station
New Delhi - 110 015
Phones : (011) 2545-3975, 2546-6019; *Fax* : (011) 2546-5926
E-mail : dkprintworld@vsnl.net
Web : www.dkprintworld.com

Printed by: Decent Books, New Delhi

Contents

Key to Transliteration

VOWELS

अ *a*	आ *ā*	इ *i*	ई *ī*	उ *u*	ऊ *ū*
(but)	(palm)	(it)	(beet)	(put)	(pool)
ऋ *ṛ*	ए *e*	ऐ *ai*	ओ *o*	औ *au*	
(rhythm)	(play)	(air)	(toe)	(loud)	

CONSONANTS

Guttural	क *ka*	ख* *kha*	ग *ga*	घ *gha*	ङ *ṅa*
	(skate)	(blockhead)	(gate)	(ghost)	(sing)
Palatal	च *ca*	छ* *cha*	ज *ja*	झ *jha*	ञ *ña*
	(chunk)	(catch him)	(john)	(hedgehog)	(bunch)
Cerebral	ट *ṭa*	ठ* *ṭha*	ड *ḍa*	ढ* *ḍha*	ण* *ṇa*
	(start)	(anthill)	(dart)	(godhead)	(under)
Dental	त *ta*	थ *tha*	द *da*	ध* *dha*	न *na*
	(path)	(thunder)	(that)	(breathe)	(numb)
Labial	प *pa*	फ* *pha*	ब *ba*	भ *bha*	म *ma*
	(spin)	(philosophy)	(bin)	(abhor)	(much)
Semi-	य *ya*	र *ra*	ल *la*	व *va*	
vowels	(young)	(drama)	(luck)	(vile)	
Sibilants	श *śa*	ष *ṣa*	स *sa*	ह *ha*	
	(shove)	(bushel)	(so)	(hum)	
Others	क्ष *kṣa*	त्र *tra*	ज्ञ *jña*	ळ* *ḷ*	ॠ* *ṝ*
(*kṣatriya*)	(*triśūla*)	(*jñānī*)	(*play*)		

अं (ं) *ṁ anusvāra* (nasalisation of preceding vowel) like *saṁskṛti*

अः *visarga* = *ḥ* (aspiration of preceding vowel) like (*prātaḥ*)

ऽ *Avagraha* consonant #'consonant (like:- *ime 'vasthitā*)

Anusvāra at the end of a line is presented by m (म्) and not ṁ

* No exact English equivalents for these letters.

Introduction

Classical Indian Philosophy Reinterpreted is a collection of articles by Victoria Lysenko from the Centre for Oriental Philosophies, Russian Academy of Sciences, Moscow and Michael Hulin, former Professor of Indian and Comparative Philosophy at the University of Paris-Sorbonne (Paris-IV) — two distinguished international scholars, very much committed to the research and study of Indian philosophy and Indology. Lysenko and Hulin delivered lectures at the Centre for Sri Aurobindo Studies, Department of Philosophy, Jadavpur University as Visiting Faculties during December 2005. This volume, the subsequent outcome of the series of lectures delivered at the Centre by these two remarkable scholars, consists of articles providing exegesis, analysis and reinterpretation of some basic concepts such as *paramāṇu* (atom), *sāmānya* (universal), *ahaṁkāra* (ego-principle) and *karma* from the perspective of classical Indian philosophy especially from the point of view of schools like the Nyāya-Vaiśeṣikas, Sāṁkhyas, and the Buddhists. The considerable importance of this study lies, as we shall see, in presenting Indian concepts from a comparative perspective as well.

Victoria Lysenko in the article, "Atomistic Formulations in Indian Thought" traces back the idea of atoms as the ultimate constituent of things prevailing among the Greeks and Indians long before the discovery of atoms by scientists. Philosophers, scientists and common people as well try to give answer to the question regarding the creation of this wonderful world. The doctrine of atomism, in brief, is also an attempt to answer this question. In India the atomism was embraced by different schools of thinkers including the Jainas, the Buddhists, the Nyāya-Vaiśeṣikas, the Sāṁkhya-Yogīs and the Madhva Vedāntins, though they had considerable differences of opinion regarding the nature of atoms. In developing Indian versions of atomism Lysenko provides exegetical analysis of different views and arguments in defence of atomism by referring to *Tattvārthādhigama-Sūtra* of Umāsvāti, *Abhidharmakoṣa* of Vasubandhu, *Padārthadharmasaṁgraha* of Praśastapāda, *Brahama-Sūtra-Bhāṣya* of Śaṅkara, and *Nyāya-Sūtra* of Gotama. Among the ancient philosophical traditions apart from the Greeks and classical Indian thinkers we hardly come across any versions of atomism. Lysenko has her own way of answering this: in Sanskrit language or Greek language the construction of a complex linguistic structure proceeds from the combination of simpler linguistic units. These simple linguistic units served as models in any explanation; hence, in accounting for the construction of complex things of the world, it is presumed by Lysenko, these thinkers depended on the same pattern of explanation. Lysenko observes that certain pre-scientific theoretical thinking in terms of constructs like whole and part, cause and effect, essence and appearance, one and many might have given these thinkers insight to posit atoms in their explanation of the world.

In the article, "Origin of the Idea of Universals — Vaiśeṣika or Vyākaraṇa," she attempts to trace the very beginning of this metaphysical idea of the universal. She very rightly considers the debate regarding the nature of the universals to be one of the important issues in Indian metaphysics. The very starting point of her discussion is the question regarding the difference, if any, between the idea of general or common property as Grammarians knew it, and the idea of universals as an independent category of the Vaiśeṣikas. The problem centring around universals is a perennial problem of philosophy in the West and in Indian philosophy as well. It has been hotly debated whether cowness is something over and above individual cows, or cowness extends over the class of all cows, or cowness is just a name? The Grammarians, as has been pointed out, accept that generic properties are unchangeable and individuals are changeable. But they do not subscribe to the view that general properties are eternal. In the scheme of the Grammarians existence as such is not differentiated from the existence of individual things and processes. In the Vaiśeṣika framework, as Victoria elaborates, since there is a necessary correspondence between words and things they designate, there must be a thing corresponding to the generic term *sattā* — some essence that exists in things (*in re*), but is not identical to them. Very meticulously following *Vaiśeṣika-Sūtra*s and their explanations Lysenko attempts to corroborate her analysis.

Michael Hulin's article, "The Ego-principle (Ahaṁkāra) as a key Concept in the Sāṁkhyakārikā" is an attempt to throw light on another pivotal metaphysical idea. Hulin undertakes this arduous task of interpreting the Sāṁkhya philosophy and this evidently shows his interest for the subject concerned. The Sāṁkhya philosophy, as he admitted, is a source of inspiration — both intellectual and spiritual — to him. He does not join hand with those who dump the Sāṁkhya philosophy as a dead "stuff" or as an instance of mere "scholarly" theoretical knowledge. Hulin is quite expressive in stating the kind of interpretation that he would prefer, that is interpreting a system from inside, in explaining the position of the Sāṁkhya school of thinkers. The Sāṁkhya school of thinkers upholds the duality of *puruṣa* and *prakṛti*, as the opposition between subjectivity and objectivity. How to bridge this gap between the *puruṣa* and *prakṛti*? The Sāṁkhya scheme of duality also entails a kind of demarcation between cosmic aspect of *tattva*s and psychological aspect of *tattva*s. The Sāṁkhya philosophy seems to be incomprehensible to those who are guided by the Cartesian idea that mind and body are diametrically opposite. Hulin discusses in detail the Sāṁkhya concept of *ahaṁkāra* or ego principle with reference to its specific function, called *abhimāna* and refers to commentaries by Vācaspati Miśra and also to other texts. According to the classical Sāṁkhya texts the *ahaṁkāra* is the product of *buddhi*; there is some difference of opinion among the Sāṁkhya thinkers as to the actual role of *ahaṁkāra*. Questions are raised as to the real utility of *ahaṁkāra* at the psychological level of the man. However, Hulin's way of interpreting the system from the inside throws some light by removing the apparent contradiction between the psychological and cosmic aspects of *tattva*s.

"The Difficult Task of Hitting the Mean: Aristotle's Mean (Mesotes) and Buddha's Middle Path (Majjhima Pacipada)" is another important article, the contributor of which is Victoria Lysenko. She has taken into consideration apparently two similar concepts from two different philosophers. Aristotle's concern with metaphysics was very direct; he considered metaphysics as the study of "existence" as the study of "being *qua* being." But for Buddha ultimate metaphysical enquiry was useless for he was concerned with the practical goal of liberation. Notwithstanding this difference in approach of that of Aristotle and Buddha, Victoria discovers a close bond between these two thinkers. Both of them realized how difficult it was to reach the Ideal — for Aristotle it was ethical and for Buddha it was religious. Both of these thinkers understood that the attainment of the ideal is linked up with the mean or the middle, and for this reason it has been said that the objective of philosophy is the difficult task of hitting the mean.

Hulin discusses various aspects of *karma* and its relation to other domains. *Karma* is a peculiarly Indian concept and it is dominantly one of the metaphysical concepts. In the Indian metaphysics the concept of *karma* has a definite role to play. In discussing Indian atomism, we have seen that Victoria Lysenko pointed out that the idea of *adṛṣṭa* or unseen kārmic force is responsible for the configuration of things produced from atoms. But the concept of *karma,* its consequences and laws relating to *karma* have deep ethical connotations as well. In the article "Reinterpretations of Karman in Contemporary Western Societies" Hulin gives an account of belief in the transmigration of soul from body to body through rebirths. The author discusses about the resurgence of the belief in reincarnation in the twentieth century especially among the Western thinkers. He analyses in detail various implications of the notion of reincarnation especially as it is understood in the tradition of Christianity to compare and contrast it with the Indian notion of transmigration.

In his article on "Karman — Ethics and Soteriology" Hulin brings out presuppositions of *karman* doctrine. He observes that the notion of *karma* has an ethical connotation for good rebirths are associated with rewarding moral actions and bad rebirths with punishing immoral ones. In this article he discusses in detail the functioning of *karma* as a mechanism of retribution. The author also tries to show it is practically impossible to explain exactly the working of *karma* as a retributive mechanism. He raises questions about the traditional fatalistic interpretation of *karma* also.

The other paper in this volume is "Karman in the Āyurveda" in which it has been discussed how traditional Indian medicine reconciles the principle of kārmic causality with empirical facts. In the Āyurveda there are discussions about the various types of diseases and their ways of treatment. The discussion begins with the interesting question: If *karma* determines all aspects of life, including its fortune and misfortune, in terms of health, wealth and other items, what role does medicine — that is the diagnosis, prevention and treatment of diseases — play? How to relate kārmic causality with incurable diseases, psychological disorders and epidemics? Most of these issues are included in Hulin's discussion.

The last article in this volume is by Victoria Lysenko; the title of the essay is "Classical Indian Philosophy in the Perspective of Cultural Studies : Sketching a New Approach." In this article the objective of the author is very transparent. Lysenko once again rekindles the debate whether Indian philosophy is a genuine philosophy. Broadly speaking, she highlights two sorts of approaches regarding what philosophy is: The first approach, as she characterizes, is based on taking any philosophy in the light of genus-species relationship. In this approach one may begin with a definition of philosophy derived either from Aristotle, Descartes or Hegel as the premise and try to derive features of Indian philosophy from it. The second approach consists in looking at philosophy not from some pre-conceived generic of philosophy but looking at philosophy from the cultural traditions in which it grows.

Essays in this volume are reflections of sincere endeavours to interpret Indian philosophical ideas as much authentically as possible. However, I believe that difference of opinion, if any arises, in understanding or interpreting concepts that are discussed in this volume, would not prevent anybody from appreciating the enormity of the task rendered by these two scholars to enliven classical Indian philosophy.

Indrani Sanyal
Director, Centre for Sri Aurobindo Studies
and Professor, Department of Philosophy,
Jadavpur University, Kolkata

1

Atomistic Formulations in Indian Thought

Victoria Lysenko

> IF, in some cataclysm, all of scientific knowledge were to be destroyed, and only one sentence passed on to the next generations of creatures, what statement would contain the most information in the fewest words? I believe it is the ATOMIC HYPOTHESIS (or the atomic FACT, or whatever you wish to call it) that ALL THINGS ARE MADE OF ATOMS — little particles that move around in perpetual motion, attracting each other when they are a little distance apart, but repelling upon being squeezed into one another. In that one sentence, you will see, there is an ENORMOUS amount of information about the world, if just a little imagination and thinking are applied.
>
> — Richard Feynman, *The Feynman Lectures on Physics*, lecture 1, p. 2.

I've chosen this well-known statement of Richard Feynman, one of the greatest modern physicists, not because it may have any relation to certain aspects of ancient Indian atomism, but because I would like to underline, to make more evident, the importance of the atomistic ideas for the development of theoretical thinking in general. How was it possible that long before the experimental discovery of atom, long before the a beginnings of the quantum physics with its theories and sophisticated equipment, in the two great civilizations of antiquity — Greek and Indian, there arose the idea of the ultimate constitutive part of things? If we suppose that it was a result of the observation on some general modes of human activity like constructing something from parts, for example a house or an altar from bricks, or on the destruction of things up to some further indivisible parts, then why this idea did not arise in other civilizations, like Egypt or Mesopotamia or China with their highly sophisticated construction techniques? That makes us assume that the presuppositions of this idea may be of mental order rather than of purely practical order.

What ancient India had in common with Ancient Greece concerning this kind of presuppositions? The first thing that comes to mind is their common Indo-European substrate, rather similar principles of construction of their respective languages — the Sanskrit and the Greek. We know that Democritus directly referred to the letters as an image of atoms. Though Indian tradition was mainly an oral one, and I did not till now find in it any similarly clear parallels between atoms and phonemes, this common linguistic background may be nevertheless quite important. I can refer to the well-known fact — one of the Sanskrit Vaiśeṣika texts containing the idea of atom was translated into Chinese language as early as in fifth century of Common Era, but it has not produced any impact on the Chinese thought, there was no place in it for this kind of idea, because the Chinese language was constructed in a different way from the Indo-European languages — not according to principles from letters to syllables, from syllables to parts of the word (prefixes, radicals, suffixes, endings), from words to phrases.

With this fact in mind we pass over to another important hypothesis relevant to the explication of the more or less parallel arising of atomism in Greece and in India — a possibility of influence or of borrowing. Till now we do not dispose any facts proving that Indian thinkers have borrowed this idea from Democritus or vice versa. As far as I am concerned, this kind of borrowing is hardly probable not because there were no contacts between the two civilizations, but for the reasons of more cultural order: from Indian side, it was a rather self-centric and close tradition which resisted any external influence. Thus, excluding the influence as an explanatory model, we are left with at least two series of facts. First one, some common linguistic factors — morphology of words, structure of sentence — all these facts may serve as prototypes of the idea that one can compose indefinite number of objects on the basis of some definite types of simple constitutive elements. This idea may serve as a necessary but not an indispensable condition. Otherwise, why we could not find any traces of atomism in Ancient Persia?

But what then constitutes a necessary and indispensable condition? In my opinion, it is a certain level of development of theoretical thinking, of abstract reasoning. It is absolutely inconceivable that mythological imagination or a simple common sense can produce anything like atom. What does it mean to think theoretically. It means that we are trying to understand what things are by their internal, intrinsic nature, by their essence in spite of their appearance. The atoms are something that we could not see as we are seeing ordinary things, they are not simple observable facts but pure concepts; even if we believe in their reality we can prove it only indirectly, by analogy with observable facts, like Democritus with his example of letters. But we will be mistaken if we suppose that Democritus or his teacher Leucippus has just invented their theory of atoms. When I said about a certain level of theoretical thinking I had in mind that certain philosophical problems were already not only posed but received different interpretations and resolutions.

What these problems are? Whole and part, cause and effect, essence and appearance, one and many. It is often supposed that in Greek philosophy, Democritus' theory of atoms and void was a reaction to counter Parmenides idea of one and singular immutable eternal being and his claim that the multiplicity of existing things, their changing forms and motions, are but an appearance. To account for the multiplicity and change of physical phenomena, Democritus conceived of the Void as an infinite space in which an infinite number of atoms were moving. These atoms are eternal and invisible; small, and their size cannot be diminished (hence the name atomon, or "indivisible"); they are without pores and differing only in shape, arrangement, position, and magnitude. As an ideal object an atom is easy to manipulate, in that way it has become an important constitutive element in the mental pictures of the real processes. We may perhaps say that the idea of the atomic structure was one of the first theoretical explanatory models in the history of mankind having a universal expository power.

If we know for certain that Greek atomism arose around sixth-fifth centuries BCE, turning to India we find ourselves in a total chronological uncertainty. We have nothing or almost nothing which permits us to date the beginnings of Indian atomism. The principal difficulty with dating in India is due to the fact that the body of knowledge in different areas was transmitted orally and the majority of texts that were preserved from these times were exclusively the oral texts.

Even if we will establish that this or that mention of *paramāṇu* (in sense of atom) in some text which reached us was the earliest one comparing with some other texts, we could not conclude from that that it was really earlier, because before their fixation in a written form all these texts were a part of the oral tradition which could have been in existence over a long period of time.

But in comparison to Greece, in India, the atomistic ideas were much more widespread. At least three traditions of Indian thought have their own versions of the atomism: Jainism, Buddhism and Vaiśeṣika. In later period it is due to Vaiśeṣika that some other orthodox schools, that is, schools which accepted the authority of the Vedas, have introduced the atomic conception in their world pictures (first of all the Nyāya, then the Mīmāṁsā, the Sāṁkhya, the Yoga and even the Vedānta in its Madhva's dualistic version). If we compare the three forms of atomism developed in India with one another, the most ancient among them seems to be the Jaina one. The Jaina atoms have preserved an evidently archaic character. The Sanskrit word for atom is *paramāṇu* — super fine, super thin, super minute. The Jaina *paramāṇu* are not divided in classes according to the classes of elements, like in other Indian schools. They contain all the properties of gross objects but in their undeveloped form. What is the most important about these atoms concerns not so much their indivisibility as in Greece, as their minuteness or subtleness (the adjective *aṇu* means thin, subtle, minute). Being the smallest unit of matter (*pudgala* — not sentient matter), individual *paramāṇu* is nevertheless devoid of impenetrability. In the most important Jaina Sanskrit philosophical work, composed early in the Common Era, the *Tattvārthādhigamasūtra* by Umāsvāti, it is said that the infinite number of *paramāṇu* could be found at one and the same spot just as the infinite number of light beams could intersect at one and the same point of space. Two *paramāṇu* can form a combination which is held together by the force of cohesion due to the fact that one of them possesses viscosity and the other dryness. These are the most important characteristics of the Jaina atomism.

Quite probably around the same time (from third century BCE up to the first century of Common Era) besides the Jaina atomism some Buddhist atomistic formulations were also developed along with development of the Buddhist philosophy. We can find them in the famous *Abhidharmakośa* of Vasubandhu (a text of the fourth century of the Common Era), being itself a compendium of *Mahāvibhāṣā*, the Buddhist text, composed around the first century BCE. The Buddhist atomism is even more vague than the Jaina one. The Buddhists stress above all the momentary and changeable character of their atoms. As they make no distinction between the substance and its qualities, their atoms are classified into 14 classes or types, distributed among the three larger groups: the atoms of the great elements (*mahābhūta*) : earth, water, fire, wind, the atoms of the qualities of these elements (atoms of smell, taste, colour, etc.) and even the atoms of organs of sense (smell, taste, vision, etc.). These heteroclite atoms cannot form any regular stable "molecules," but only temporary aggregates (*skandha*), divisible by 7. In this way, the Buddhist thinkers explain the changeable and unstable nature of reality.

But the most elaborate and sophisticated atomistic doctrine belongs to Vaiśeṣika. The origins of this school were quite obscure. It is often supposed that in its earliest forms it was developed independently of the Vedas, but in the course of time its thinkers were got into the sphere of the Brahmanical influence. The *Vaiśeṣikasūtras*, the basic text of this tradition (codified around the first century of the Common Era) mentions the atoms quite optionally, incidentally as though we have affair with something obvious and self-evident. One may have an impression that in Ancient India the atomistic ideas were so universally known that there was no need to prove or explain them. Only in the sixth century of our era the commentator of the *Vaiśeṣikasūtras*, Praśastapāda, in his *Padārthadharmasaṁgraha* presented this doctrine in a more clear way, but still without any attempt to systematically prove the existence of atoms. Nevertheless, these proofs existed and we learn about them from outside of the Vaiśeṣika tradition. The first of these proofs possesses pure logical character. It consists in establishing the atom as a means to stop short the regress to infinity in the process of division (I will return to it later on).

Now, I would like to turn your attention to the second proof. Though we know about it from the commentary of the great Indian philosopher Śaṁkara to the *Brahmasūtra* and that text was composed in the eighth century of our era, much later than the *Nyāyasūtra* (further on *NS*) where the first proof was announced, we have some rather substantial reasons to believe that Śaṁkara referred to some early Vaiśeṣika text that did not come to us.

Śaṁkara presents the arising of the Vaiśeṣika atomistic doctrine in the following way (I quote from his *Brahmasūtrabhāṣya*, the II.2.12):

> We see that all ordinary substances which consist of parts as, for instance, pieces of cloth originate from the substances connected with them by the relation of inherence, as for instance, threads, conjunction co-operating (with the parts to form the whole). We thence draw the general conclusion that whatever consists of parts has originated from those

> substances with which it is connected by the relation of inherence, conjunction cooperating. That thing now at which the distinction of the whole and parts stops and which marks the limit of division into minuter parts is the atom. — This whole world, with its mountains, oceans, and so on, is composed of parts; it has a beginning and an end; an effect could not be assumed without a cause; therefore the atoms are the cause of the world.

What can attract our attention here is exactly this very philosophical way to deduce the existence of atom from the generalized observations on arising the object from its part. Thus the postulation of atom was closely connected with two main philosophical problems that is of whole and its parts, at one hand, and of effect and its cause or causes, at the other. It were mainly these two problems which, perhaps, gave birth to the Vaiśeṣika atomism and which at the same time put under the doubt its coherence while discovering its weakest points.

Let us now turn to the Nyāya proof of existence of atom. In the *Nyāyasūtra*, three possibilities of division of whole into parts are examined (*NS*, 4.2.15-17): the first one is a division till the full destruction, or rather dissolution of things (*pralaya*). But that will mean that all things consist of *pralaya* (dissolution) and they simply do not exist (*NS*, 4.2.15). The other possibility is an infinite division (*NS*, 4.2.17); in that case the very large object as well as the Dyad (molecule of two atoms) would both consist of endless number of particles (the famous paradox of the Mount Meru and a grain which would consist of the equally innumerable parts). The third possibility is the only valid one — neither destruction, nor regress to the infinity is admissible, because there remains the Atom which is something (a physical object) which has no parts to which it may be divisible. As the a commentator puts it, "When a clod of earth comes to be divided into smaller and smaller pieces, that point at which the division ceases, and then when there is nothing smaller, is what we call *paramāṇu* (the atom)" (Vārttika to *NS*, 4.2.16). But the polemics which follows this *sūtra* shows that the fact of being something material, even if this atom is of the smallest dimension, is logically hardly compatible with being without constituting parts. In other words, the purely physical character of atom threatens its metaphysical status as an ultimate cause and as the originator of all composed things.

The first argument is as follows: There can be no such thing as the indivisible eternal atom, because it is surely permeated by *ākāśa*, ether; both inside and outside the Atom must be surrounded by *ākāśa* and permeated by it; and being so permeated, it must be made up of parts, and being made up of parts, it must be transient (*NS*, 4.2.18). Otherwise, *ākāśa* would not be all-penetrating (*NS*, 4.2.19).

The other argument concerns the way the atoms are connected with one another. Because the atoms are capable of conjunction they must be made up of component parts (*NS*, 4.2.24). That is, explains the commentator,

> when an Atom comes between two other atoms and becomes conjoined to them, it brings about separation between them; and from this separation it is inferred that the intervening atom is conjoined, in its fore-part, with the atom lying behind it, and, in its aft-part, with the atom appearing in front of it; and these fore and aft-parts are "the component parts" of the Atom. Similarly when the atom becomes conjoined in all its parts, it must be regarded as having component parts all over.

In other words, if we assume that atom may enter in conjunction with other atoms, we must agree that it has its component parts, but if it has its component parts, it is no longer the atom, the smallest and further indivisible corpuscular. This is a kind of difficulty that arises in all the forms of the philosophical atomism as distinct from the scientific one. As a matter of fact, if we consider an atom to be a kind of a physical body, we may always put under a question its indivisibility, but if we try to see in it a kind of mathematical point, we could not explain in what way these points may form a physical body. We know very well that addition of mathematical points is still a mathematical point and no increase of physical volume could be obtained in this way, because these points, unlike the atoms, are devoid of impenetrability. That means that two atoms cannot occupy one and the same place, but as regards the mathematical points, even if they are innumerable nothing prevents them from occupying one and the same point of space.

Facing this kind of difficulty the Greek and after them the Arab atomists try to distinguish between the real physical and the imaginable mental divisibility. According to some fragments, Democritus draws distinction between atoms, on one side, and logically or mentally discernible parts of atoms, or the ameros, on the other side. This division has become much clearer with Epicures. For Democritus, the indivisibility of the atoms does not entail the minimality of their size. As we know, the atoms of Democritus are differing not only by their forms, but also by their size. On the contrary, the atomism of the Vaiśeṣika and Nyāya traditions is based on the idea of the minimal size of the atom which is called *parimaṇḍala* spherical. The *parimaṇḍala* is a kind of ideal form which is indivisible in logical, or in metaphysical sense. It neither generates the other forms, nor is generated by them. It is a pure metaphysical cause.

But the Vaiśeṣika atom is nevertheless not a pure geometrical figure, it is the smallest physical body endowed with the properties or qualities of the great element (*mahābhūta*) to which it belongs. Thus, the Vaiśeṣikas classify the atoms into four main groups: the atoms of earth (*pṛthvī*), the atoms of water (*āp*), the atoms of fire (*tejas*) and the atoms of wind (*vāyu*). The European atomism, in its strict sense, beginning from Greeks, is characterized not only by indivisibility of atoms, but also by their qualitative identity (they are distinct only in shape, size, and motion). In India, on the contrary, the atoms were quantitatively the same (all of them were spherical), but qualitatively diverse. The atoms of earth possess smell, taste, colour, touch, the atoms of water — taste, colour, touch, the atoms of fire — colour, touch, and the atoms of wind — touch only.

But as to individual, separate atom the question arises whether it is endowed with qualities. Till now, I could not find the direct answer to this question in any of the Vaiśeṣika texts I examined, but by some indirect signs we may conclude that the physical qualities of the separate atoms were somehow present but none of them were manifested to the point to reach our senses. What we perceive as smell, taste, etc. is well and truly the taste and the smell of atoms, but only when they are in combinations, in "molecules." The Vaiśeṣikas talked most often about two kinds of combinations — dyads and triads (*dvyāṇuka* and *tryāṇuka*), but in what way they were formed? That brings us to one of the most complicated issues of the Vaiśeṣika atomism — the formation of perceptible objects from imperceptible atoms.

At the beginning of the world cycle (*sṛṣṭi*) all the atoms were in their non-combined isolated state. The most sophisticated argumentation was elaborated by Praśastapāda's commentators Śrīdhara, Vyomaśiva and Udayana. As maintained by Śrīdhara, a single atom cannot be productive, because if it could, it would produce its effects eternally and these effects would be indestructible. Nor could the combination of three atoms be regarded as productive, because being perceptible and thus made up of parts, a *tryāṇuka* has to be equally made up of constitutive parts which were in their turn effects. Therefore, its parts were *dvyāṇuka* (a substance-effect), but not three single atoms (substances-causes). And finally, two dyads do not produce perceptible things because it is not a number two, but number three which is productive of a large measure of things.

We can see here a general problem pertaining to metaphysics in general, regardless of its concrete forms, Western or Eastern. I refer to a problem of transition from Metaphysical to Physical, from One to Many, from Eternal to Transient, from Absolute to Phenomenal, etc. The metaphysical *prima causa* seems to be too pure and too perfect to initiate a production. Actually, the Absolute in metaphysics cannot be nothing else than a sterile entity, incapable of production. To be productive One needs something which is more than One, the Pure needs something, say, not so pure, like for instance *māyā* (principle of illusion), or *prakṛti* (matter), or even *avidyā* (ignorance). Thus an implicit or explicit duality may suggest itself as the only way out from the blind alley of sterility. It is symptomatic that all metaphysical, as well as religious systems, as far as they have tried to explain the transition from any kind of Absolute to the phenomenal world, *vollens-nollens* have come to use dyads (like Self and non-Self in Fichte, matter and mind in dualist philosophical systems like that of Descartes and Sāṁkhya, etc.) and triads (Hegel's thesis, counter-thesis, synthesis, Hindu Trimūrti, Christian Trinity, etc.).

Though the Vaiśeṣika atomism is not a monistic system it is still a metaphysical system; that is why we find here the same problem. Any atomicstic theory can be interpreted as an attempt to reconcile the thesis of the unity and immutability of being with the fact that the senses observe multiplicity and change. Democritus tried to reduce all the observable qualitative diversity of objects to the quantitative differences between the atoms. In Vaiśeṣika, all kinds of properties of elements have their origin in the appropriate kinds of atoms. But that does not mean that a singular atom has some particular properties, say a single separate atom can possess the properties of sugar. The sugar becomes sugar only at the level of the *tryāṇuka*, the triad. Why the *tryāṇuka* and not the *dvyāṇuka*, the dyad?

As follows from the Vaiśeṣika viewpoint, the minute size of a single atom cannot bring into being a magnitude of gross things, because an addition of the ultimately small measures may give the increase only of the same small measure. But as the *aṇu* is already the limit of the minuteness which could not be surpassed, the size of a dyad continues to be as minute (*aṇu*) as the size of a single atom. As the Vaiśeṣikas did not see any quantitative difference between the size of one and of two atoms, they did not recognize the different degrees of minuteness with regard to a single atom and a dyad. The triad was held to be a combination not of three singular atoms, but of three dyads and only this triad and neither dyads, nor single atoms, were endowed with a capacity to bring about the gross things. Are we dealing here with a kind of Pythagorean ontology of numbers, which endows them with the capacity to produce things? What we can say with a certain certitude is that the number three is associated in the Vaiśeṣika's thought with the minimal plurality (*bahutva*) and what is even more important — with the possibility of perception. We begin to see things starting with the triads composing of three dyads. The favourite Vaiśeṣika's natural example of triad is *tresareṇu* — a mote of dust moving in a sun-beam.

Thus, our sugar becomes sugar only on the level of triads. If we divide it into its component parts, the smallest possible particles will be the triads. But what about further parts, which are not perceptible (we can easily imagine that the division of the sugar material could be continued beyond the threshold of perceptibility)? Do the atoms and the dyads of sugar possess the same sweetness and whiteness as our "gross piece" of sugar? I suppose that at this level, neither atoms, nor dyads have any particular properties. Our pre-sugar atoms and dyads may have some general qualities characteristic of this class of atoms — the earth atoms which have some indefinite smell, some taste, some touch, etc. In other words, they may have some possibilities, potentials of smell, taste, colour or touch.

My supposition is indirectly confirmed by Praśastapāda's commentator, when he mentions that the atoms of earth haven't any species. That means that the atoms are not divided on the basis of their belonging to species corresponding to the earth substances like class of cows, or class of pots, etc. Otherwise, they would be something like homeomeria of the Greek thinker Anaxagoras who believed the smallest parts of some things to be a kind of miniature copies of these things; thus he assumed as many qualitatively different "atoms" as there are different substances in nature.

But if the Vaiśeṣika's atoms of one class are not responsible for the diversity within this very class, how could it be explained? In other words, what was the Vaiśeṣika explanation of the structural and material diversity of this universe? To understand this problem properly, we should address ourselves to another facet of the Vaiśeṣika system — its ethics and soteriology. According to Praśastapāda this universe undergoes a cyclical emission and absorption (*sṛṣṭi* and *pralaya*). During *pralaya* there are only atoms of great elements, and souls experiencing either pleasure or pain according to their previous deeds, the traces of which were preserved in *adṛṣṭa*s — invisible forces of *karman*. It is due to these *adṛṣṭa*s that our universe at the beginning of its emission takes the same form as it had had before the *pralaya*. Thus, there is a progressive formation of the great elements and then of the living beings. All this process proceeds through *Īśvara*, the Demiurge, and with the assistance of the *adṛṣṭa*s.

According to Praśastapāda, "A multitude appears in the atoms and the dyads due to the *apekṣabuddhi* of Īśvara, and when these dyads produce effects in the form of the triads, etc. the multitude produces in them a colour along with a longness and a magnitude." Thus, along with the perceptible size, the multitude, in the form of the number "three," produces in effects (the gross things from *tresareṇu* onwards) the perceptible qualities like colour, taste, smell, etc. And this very multitude is introduced into atoms by the *apekṣabuddhi* of Īśvara. What is *apekṣabuddhi*? Literally, "depending on *buddhi*," or depending on the cognitive act. Being fundamental, the single atoms, at the beginning of the new world cycle, are nevertheless non-productive and thus in need of the *apekṣabuddhi* for their effects to be produced. One is tempted to regard the *apekṣabuddhi* as quite similar to Greek Nous, Cartesian Mind or Newtonian Reason. But in my opinion, the *apekṣabuddhi* is rather a cognitive act grasping several things at a time, and not a substantialized intellectual capacity. In the course of *sṛṣṭi*, or emission of the world, dyads are resulting out of Īśvara's simultaneous cognition of two atoms, triads — of three dyads. As for the role of the "first impulse" that compels the atoms to combine into these "molecules" it is played by the above-said *adṛṣṭa*s. Thus, during the *sṛṣṭi*, the physical universe is created according to a certain moral and religious design kept and carried on by the *adṛṣṭa*s through the time of *pralaya* (a cosmic night). The role of Īśvara, in the final analysis, is like that of Demiurges in Peaton's *Timeus;* as for the *adṛṣṭa*s, they may be compared to the *eidoi,* the original paradigm that serves Demiurges as a model of creation, or in more modern term to a kind of genetic programme for each living creature and for the whole universe.

In the normal state of universe, when its karmically determined structure is well established, Īśvara interferes not more in any process of production. It is *adṛṣṭa* or rather *adṛṣṭa*s (in plural) that play the role of, so to say, teleological factor in the production of ordinary things. What makes such a thing as a pot is not only its material, but its form as well. The Vaiśeṣika authors are talking of *vyūha* — configuration of atoms — as such form-making factor. It is mainly this configuration due to which the combinations of atoms from triads onwards may be regarded as constitutive parts of sugar or of some other particular substance. But this *vyūha* is not something spontaneous or casual, being the result of the certain *adṛṣṭa*. The *adṛṣṭa* is a quality of soul (*ātman*), a cosmo-ethical factor representing individual *karman*. How could *adṛṣṭa* as a quality of soul have something in common with production of sugar or of pots, or of any other composed thing? According to the Vaiśeṣika, our souls are *vibhu*, that means, all-pervading, omnipresent. All the universe is permeated by the infinite number of souls of all living creatures. But that does not mean that the entire universe is animated or intelligent, because the soul can serve as an animating or intelligent principle only when it is in contact with a *manas*, or internal organ, coordinator of the senses, which exists within the particular body. Outside the body our *ātman* is deprived of consciousness, but it still continues to be the support of *adṛṣṭa*s from our previous existences. Thus we can imagine that all the artefacts produced by men are determined not only by the professional capacities of their producers, but also by their *adṛṣṭa*s. As for the things produced in nature they are also influenced by the *adṛṣṭa*s. What kind of *adṛṣṭa*s? Our texts are silent on this subject, but we can suppose that these could be the *adṛṣṭa*s of men or animals which make a kind of summary formative karmic force taking part in all sorts of natural productions, like that of stones, salt, snow, etc. What we know for sure is the fact that in the Vaiśeṣika world-view, the material universe is inseparable from the moral order created and sustained by human beings; it is, so to say, programmed by the human, moral factor on the most deep level of reality — that of its atomic structure.

If you ask me what the most striking feature of Indian atomism is, I would first of all mention this, so to say, antropic, or moral factor. If we compare *adṛṣṭa*s as final form-making factors with the *eidoi* (image-making) or forms of the Ancient Greece, we will see it even more clearly: for Greek thinkers, the *eidoi* as well as *atomoi* are tightly connected with individuality, uniqueness, originality, and specificity. Being direct heirs of the Ancient Greek civilization, we, Westerners, consider ourselves as individuals (the words *in-dividus* is a Latin synonym of the Greek atom). In its extreme forms the so-called social atomism appears in the tragic solitude of the Protestant self-made man or in existential estrangement of a modern man. In India, the idea of the atom never became either scientific theory, or a prototype of the social individualism. Through the *adṛṣṭa* it was always connected with the specifically Indian view of the universe as a place where living beings are involved in the incessant trial of reincarnation (*saṁsāra*) and where their actual individuality is far from being single and unique, as many other ones will follow in future existences. At the same time due to the concept of *adṛṣṭa*s Indian atomism — in much more degree than the Greek one — may serve as an example of the real confluence of physical and ethical orders (the idea of *dharma*).

See my Other Contributions to the Same Topic

"The Atomistic Theory of the Vaiśeṣika: Problems of Interpretation" in *History of Indian Philosophy: A Russian Viewpoint*, Indian Council of Philosophical Research, New Delhi, 1993, pp. 56-71.

"Atomistic Mode of Thinking as Exemplified by the Vaiśeṣika Philosophy of Number," in: *Asiatische Studien/Etudes Asiatiques*, Bern, etc. 1994, vol. XLVIII, No. 2, pp. 781-806.

"La doctrine des atomes chez Kaṇāda et Praśastapāda," *Journal Asiatique*, Paris, 1996, vol. 248, No. 1, pp. 137-58.

"The Vaiśeṣika Notions of *ākāśa* and *di*? From the Perspective of Indian Ideas of Space" in *Beyond Orientalism*, "The Work of Wilhelm Halbfass and its Impact on Indian and Cross-cultural Studies," Poznan Studies in the Philosophy of Science and Humanities, vol. 47, Amsterdam, 1996, pp. 417-47.

"The Human Body Composition in Statics and Dynamics: Āyurveda and the Philosophical schools of Vaiśeṣika and Sāṁkhya," *Journal of Indian Philosophy*, vol. 32, No. 1, 2004, pp. 31-56.

"Śaṁkara, critique du Vaiśeṣika. Une lecture de Brahmasūtrabhāṣya (II, 2, 11-17)," *Asiatische Studien/Etudes Asiatique*, LIX 2, Lousanne, 2005, pp. 533-80.

2

Origin of the Idea of Universals
Vaiśeṣika or Vyākaraṇa

Victoria Lysenko

THE origin of universals (in the scholastic sense) constitutes an intriguing issue (Halbfass' expression) of Indian studies. In this paper, I am arguing that the idea of universals, though it was largely indebted to the early grammatical tradition (especially to Patañjali), was primarily postulated not in the *Mahābhāṣya* (as some scholars believe), but in the *Vaiśeṣikasūtras* (further, *VS*).

We usually use the word "universal" for the Vaiśeṣika term *sāmānya*. However, even within the limits of Vaiśeṣika itself, the notion of universal is much larger than that of the *sāmānya* and the semantic field of the *sāmānya*, in turn, does not coincide with the meaning of the term "universal." First of all, the *VS* do not make any clear-cut semantic distinction between *sāmānya* as a noun and as an adjective, or in more philosophical terms, between *sāmānya* as a universal (in the scholastic sense) and *sāmānya* designating a general or a common property, as opposed to an individual or a specific property (*viśeṣa*). In the latter case, the *sāmānya* may form a part of the compound (of the *dvandva* type) *sāmānyaviśeṣa*, which may be translated as "general-specific factor," "universal-individual," or "genus-species" (subsumption relation). But in the *VS*, the compound word *sāmānyaviśeṣa* most likely designates a type of universals — the "specific universals" or the "inferior universals" (*aparasāmānya*) in opposition to the "highest universal" (*parasāmānya*) represented by *sattā* — the universal of existence. In my opinion, in the *VS*, *sāmānya* and *viśeṣa* are sometimes used in the sense of general (or common) and specific characteristics (*sādharmya* and *vaidharmya*) applicable to the universals themselves. In this connection, I propose a new translation of some *VS*.

In the translations of the Vaiśeṣika texts into European languages these latter connotations are usually ignored. In their pursuit of unification, the translators try to render *sāmānya* by one and the same term: either "universal," or "generic property," or "class," and *viśeṣa* as "individual," "specific" or "species" (a list of different translations of these terms may be found in Halbfass 1992: 115). Halbfass himself prefers "universal" for *sāmānya* and "particularity" for *viśeṣa*. But in his translations from the *VS* with Candrānanda commentary he finally renders *sāmānya* not only as "universal" but also as "universal factor" (Halbfass 1992: 238-46). The semantic diversity of the Vaiśeṣika term *sāmānya* was perceived by two Indian authors — Harsh Narain and Gajendragadkar. Narain makes a distinction between "the category of *sāmānya* and the ordinary similarity" (Narain 1976: 179), and Gajendragadkar — between the absolute and the relative senses of *sāmānya*: in the first case it is a universal, in the second — a general factor correlative of the particular one (*viśeṣa*) (Gajendragadkar 1988: 89).

Secondly, it is very important to take into account that the concept of universals in classical Vaiśeṣika of Praśastapāda (sixth century CE) is based on the complementarity of *sāmānya* and *viśeṣa* both as entities and as the characteristics of these entities. Their opposition lies within the idea of universals in general. This opposition explains why there are two kinds of universals — the supreme one (*parasāmānya*) and the inferior one (*aparasāmānya*). In addition to this opposition, the universal as a category (*padārtha*) is contrasted with the *antyaviśeṣa* — the "ultimate particularity" or the "ultimate specific factor" formative of the correlative category of *viśeṣa*.

The terms *sāmānya* and *jāti* in the Vyākaraṇa literature are sometimes translated as "universals."[1] I agree with Harsh Narain who thought that Patañjali himself had not formulated the concept of universals in a philosophical or ontological sense (Narain 1976: 191), but his commentators Kayaṭa and Nāgeśa read this concept into his text. That brings us to the following question: What is the difference between the idea of general or common property, as grammarians (especially Patañjali) knew it, and the idea of universals? In the theory of universals, the general property has been transformed into a kind of a self-sufficient and eternal essence included into the list of ontological entities. One may ask: is "cowness" something other than an individual "cow"?

The grammarians use the word *ākṛti*, common shape, generic form, class property[2] which is also sometimes rendered by the term "universal." In my opinion, a class property as well as the class itself are something more concrete and

---

1. The sentence *jātyākhyāyāṁ sāmānyābhidhānādaikārthyam* (1.2.58 *VMbh*, I : 229), P.S. Filliozat translates *jāti* by "gender" and *sāmānya* by "universal" (Filliozat 1980: 234). In some passages, Filliozat refers to *ākṛti* and *dravya* using the terms "universel" and "individual" (vol. 4, p. 343, notes 4-6; p. 346, notes 1-4; p. 347, notes 1, 2; p. 358, note 1 — for further references see Sharf 1996: 12-13).

2. For the detailed analysis of the different translations of the term *ākṛti* see Sharf 1996: 11-18.

empirical than universals — the first is a set of perceptible features characteristic of a class (*jāti*), for example, dewlap, hump, etc. for cow. The second presents a set of individuals endowed with these features. As for the universal "cowness," it is a kind of ontological foundation of such a set — something that gives it a different ontological status with regard to an individual entity: a cow. In other words, there arises a differentiation in ontological status between "cowness" and a "cow." The status of universals becomes an absolute measure for the status of transient and changeable individual things. Though Patañjali argues that class properties (*ākṛti*) may be unchangeable as compared with changeable individuals (*dravya*), he speaks about the permanence of these properties,[3] but not about their eternity in an ontological sense. He does not make any distinction between existence in general and the existence of individual things and processes.

It is this very distinction that we seem to find in the second part of the first book of the *Vaiśeṣikasūtras* (1.2.7-1.2.11 in Candrānanda's version, *VSC*): "That from which [arises the notion of] 'existent' with regard to substances, qualities and motions."[4] Or in the more explicit version of Śaṁkaramiśra (*VSŚ*): "Existence is that [from which arises the notion of] 'existent' with regard to substances, qualities and motions."[5] And further on: "Existence is something different from substances, qualities and motions."[6]

We are dealing here with a train of thought which is quite typical for the Vaiśeṣikas. For them, there is a one to one

3. *Vyākaraṇa-Mahābhāṣya of Patañjali* (*VMbh*), vol. I, p. 1, lines 6-10.

4. *saditi yato dravyaguṇakarmasu* ॥ — *VSC*, 1.2.7.

5. *saditi yato dravyaguṇakarmasu sā sattā* ॥ — *VSŚ*, 1.2.7.

6. *dravyaguṇakarmābhyo arthāntaraṁ sattā* ॥ — *VSC*, 1.2.8.

correspondence between things and words (concepts)[7] expressing them. Thus, they almost always have in mind a double perspective: that of words and that of the things which are their meanings. The idea that something is existent, which is expressed in the participle *sant* or *sat*, arises in our mind not because the existence is the inner property of substances, qualities and motions as such (the first three *padārtha*s of Vaiśeṣika), but because in our speech practice or word usage (*vyavahāra*) these participles are equally applicable to substances, qualities or motions. Therefore, there must be something uniting or assimilating all of them without being reduced to any of them.

One may ask whether this "something" has been derived from the conception of one exịstence as occurring in different types of entities, as Harsh Narain suggests (Narain 1976: 160)? I prefer to think that the universal of existence arises in Vaiśeṣika as a result of the double perspective mentioned above: the overall account of what there is (as Halbfass has shown in Halbfass 1992) in strict conformity with what we can think and say about it, that is with linguistic usage and language structure (the principle of correspondence between words and things). If we say *A* is "existent" (*sant*), *B* is "existent," it is namely this linguistic as well as cognitive fact, and not a proper nature of *A* or *B*, that is expressed by the collective noun *sattā*. That may mean that a universal is above all a referent, a meaning of the generic term, like *sattā* However, as there is a necessary correspondance between words and the things they designate, there must be a "thing" corresponding to the generic term *sattā* — some essence that exists in things (*in re*), but is not identical to them: if things are

---

7. In Indian thought, there was no clear-cut distinction between words and notions or thoughs, expressed by words.

changeable and perishable the universals must be eternal and immutable (*ante re*). The fact that the *sattā* constitutes something different from things in which it resides is confirmed by the idea that universals are supposed to be in the relation of inherence (*samavāya*) with individual substances, qualities and motions. The relation of *samavāya* is possible only in that case when we are dealing with different entities as relation involves two things related to each other. Thus I believe that existence, *sattā*, in the early and even in the classical Vaiśeṣika may be regarded as a universal of existence rather than as Being of European philosophy.

With that supposition in mind, let us return to our analysis of the *VS*: the next *sūtra*s (1.2.9-1.2.11) explain in what sense existence (or rather the universal of existence) is different from substances, qualities and motions. "[The universal of existence could not be] a substance because of its possessing of (or residing in) a single substance."[8] According to Candrānanda, a substance is either produced by many parts that are themselves substances (*anekadravya*), or not produced at all (*adravya* — not produced from *dravya*) or eternal, like atom, *ākāśa, ātman*.[9] No single substance could be the cause of another substance. What does *ekadravyatva* — literally the property of possessing one substance — mean with regard to the universal of existence? In my opinion, it may mean that existence as a *summum genus* resides in individual substances taken one by one and not in all of them collectively. Any individual substance, as well as quality or motion is a substrate or a support (*āśraya*) of the universal *sattā*. Further on, the *VS* argue that the universal of existence "is not a quality or a motion,

8. *ekadravyavattvānna dravyam* ॥ — *VSC*, 1.2.9.

9. *dravyamadravyaṁ paramāṇvākāśādi kāraṇadravyābhāvāt, anekadravyaṁ sattā samavāyikāraṇadravyayuktvāt. Sattā punaḥ parisamāptyā vartamānaikadravyavattvānna dravyam.*

because it exists in qualities and motions."[10] Vaiśeṣika formulated a sort of anti-reflexive or anti-regressive rule to prevent the regress to infinity (*anavasthā*). According to this rule, a quality cannot possess another quality[11] and a motion cannot possess another motion (one cannot colour a colour, one cannot put a motion into motion), therefore if existence is in qualities, it could not be a quality, if it is in motions it could not be a motion. This fact constitutes the first argument in favour of the otherness of the universal of existence in relation to substances, qualities and motions.

The second argument amounts to the idea that the universal of existence is not reducible to substances, qualities or motions, "because of the absence [in it] of *sāmānyaviśeṣa*, or specific universals."[12] Candrānanda explains that if the *sattā* is either substance, or quality or motion, then such specific universals as the "substantiality" would reside in the universal of existence together with substances, qualities and motions.[13] In other words, there would be a total mixture of things and universals. And also a violation of the other important Vaiśeṣika rule according to which the universal cannot contain other universals or be contained in it (*VSC*, 8.5). That is the universal of the higher order contains no lower universals but only concrete things.[14] In the next sequence of the *sūtras*, these two

10. *guṇakarmasu ca bhāvānna karma na guṇaḥ* ॥ — *VSC*, 1.2.10, *VSŚ*, 1.2.9.

11. *VSC*, I.1.15; VII.2.5;VII; VIII.8.

12. *sāmānyaviśeṣābhāvācca* ॥ — *VSC*, 1.2.11 ; *VSS*, 1.2.10.

13. *yadi sattādravyādināmanyatamā syādevaṁ dravyadiṣviva sattāyāmapi dravyatvādayaḥ sāmānyaviśeṣā varteran. tasmānna sattā dravyaguṇakarmāni* ॥ — Commentary to *VSC*, 1.2.11.

14. This restriction does not exist in Bhartṛhari's conception of universals, where universals can contain other universals — the idea of universal of universals (for instance, *Jātisamuddeśa*, 3.1.9-10)

arguments (the inherence or occurrence in something and the absence of the specific universals) are used in order to demonstrate that substantiality could not be reduced to substance,[15] qualityness to qualities,[16] motionness to motion.[17] And because these *sūtra*s are evidently symmetrical with the previous ones, we can conclude that a lower universal, just like the universal of existence, is something different from the thing in which it resides.

Praśastapāda proves the accuracy of this interpretation by referring to the analogy between the universal of existence and the dark-blue substance (*nīladravya*) or simply dark-blue paint:

> As in the case of a number of totally different things, such as pieces of leather, of cloth, of blanket and so forth — if all of them are connected with the dark-blue substance, with regard to each of these we have the notion 'this is dark-blue,' 'this is dark-blue,' in the same manner, in case of the totally different categories, substance, quality and motion, we find that with regard to each of them we have the notion that 'it exists,' and this all-inclusive notion could not but be

15. "Substanceness has (already) been established by (the criterion) 'occurrence is single (ultimate) substances'" (*ekadravyavattvena dravyatvam uktam* ॥ — *VSC*, I.2.12 — Halbfass's translation). "And also by (criterion) 'there is no specific universal (inherent in it)'" (*sāmānyaviśeṣābhāvena ca* ॥ — *VSC*, I.2.13. Halbfass' translation).

16. "Qualityness is established because (of the fact that) it exists in qualities" (*guṇe bhāvād guṇatvam uktam* ॥ — *VSC*, I.2.14. Halbfass's translation). "Also, by (the criterion) 'there is no specific universal (inherent in it)'" (*sāmānyaviśeṣabhāvena ca* ॥ — *VSC*, I.2.15).

17. "Motionness is established because (of the fact that) it exists in motions" (*karmāṇi bhāvāt karmatvam uktam* ॥ — *VSC*, I.2.16, Halbfass's translation). "Also, by (the criterion) 'that there is no specific universal (inherent in it)'" (*sāmānyaviśeṣabhāvena ca* ॥ — *VSC*, I.2.17).

> due to something apart from the three categories themselves, and this something is what we call *sattā*.
>
> — revised translation of G. Jha.[18]

I have already called *sāmānya* "something," or some sort of essence, and it seems to me that Praśastapāda had the same intuition in mind when he assimilates the *sāmānya* with the dark-blue substance. As for the rule formulated in the *VS*, 1.2.8, it is further used as a model for the demonstration of the otherness (*arthāntaratva*) of *samavāya* with regard to substances, qualities and notions (*VSC*, 7.2.30; *VSS*, 7.2.27).

I believe that the absence in Vaiśeṣika of the explicit ontological thematization of being (discussed by Halbfass) is due to the fact that existence (*sattā*) is considered (at least from the *VS* onwards) mainly as *parasāmānya* (the supreme universal). Thus, the ontological speculation begins not with the general notion of being as such, but with the universal of existence. It is a historical point which marks the appearance of the concept of universals as distinct from the concept of genus and species, or generic form (class property) developed in the Vyākaraṇa. Commentators of the Grammatical and the Nyāya traditions tried to attribute to Patañjali as well as to Gautama a conception of universals in the manner of Vaiśeṣika, and those translators and scholars who followed them have made the same mistake. That resulted in a complete confusion and even identification of universals with "genus" and "species" like in natural kinds, as in Potter's *Encyclopedia of Indian Philosophies* (Potter 1977: 134). But there is a considerable

18. [363] *yathā parasparaviśiṣṭeṣu carmavastrakambalādiṣu ekasmān nīladravyābhisambandhān nīlaṁ nīlaṁ iti pratyayānuvṛttiḥ tathā parasparaviśiṣṭeṣu dravyaguṇakarmasv aviśiṣṭā sat sad iti pratyayānuvṛttiḥ, sā cārthāntarād bhavitum arhati-iti, yad tad arthāntaraṁ sā satteti siddhā* ||

difference between them which must be taken into consideration. In the case of "genera" or "classes," we are dealing with a number of individuals composing a class on the basis of some properties common to all of them (*ākṛti*), but in the case of universals, we have to do with some essences or entities different from the categories of substance, quality and motion, as well as from individual things themselves. Otherwise it would be impossible for the universals to be connected with things with the help of the *samavāya* relation, or inherence.

If we accept the understanding of the *sattā* as a universal of existence, that will lead us to a reinterpretation of some *VS*. Let us examine the very important *sūtra* 1.2.4 *bhāva sāmānyam eva* (*VSC*). Halbfass translated it as "Existence is a universal only," Nandalal Sinha : "Existence is only a genus." Taking into account that in the *VS, bhāva* is a synonym of *sattā*, and *sattā* is the supreme universal, the term *sāmānya* here, as I think, may be a characteristic of the universal rather than the universal itself, otherwise the *sūtra* will be tautological, something like: "the universal of existence is a universal." So my translation of the two versions of this *sūtra* runs as follow: "[The universal] of existence is a general factor only" or in Śaṅkaramiśra's version: "[The universal] of existence is a general factor only, because it serves only as a basis for inclusion (*anuvṛtti*)."[19]

What in this case will the translation of the previous *sūtra*: *sāmānyaḥ viśeṣa iti budhyapekṣam* (1.2.3) be? This *sūtra* attracts the attention of scholars because of the possibility to see in it the evidence in favour of the conceptualistic and even of the

---

19. *bhāvo' nuvṛtter eva hetutvāt sāmānyam eva* ॥ — *VSŚ*, I.2.4. Nanda Lal Sinha, "Existence, being the cause of assimilation only, is only a Genus."

nominalistic position of the early Vaiśeṣika (see Narain 1976: 209 and Nozava 1994: 837). Narain himself translates it as follows: "[That this is] *sāmānya* and [this is] *viśeṣa* is dependent upon understanding" (Narain 1976: 208). Halbfass proposes another translation: "Depending on (the mode of) cognition (*buddhyapekṣa*) (the universal appears as) universal or specific factor"[20] (Halbfass 1992: 239). It is namely in this case that he translates *sāmānya* and *viśeṣa* as characteristics of universals — universal factor and specific factor. But in the next *sūtras* he returns to his initial translation — "universal" (1.2.4). "Existence (*bhāva*) is a universal only" (1.2.5). "Substanceness, qualityness, and motionness are universals as well as specific factors" (Halbfass 1992: 239).

Thus we have two interpretations. The first one is that of Halbfass (and also of Nozava) based on understanding *sāmānya* and *viśeṣa* as "universals" and "specific factors" which in itself is not quite convincing because, strictly speaking, the terms "universals" and "specific factors," cannot be opposed or distinguished in this manner. What is really different from universals are not the specific factors, *viśeṣa* (for they may refer to specific universals), but the *antyaviśeṣa*, or ultimate particularities. However, we are not dealing here with *antyaviśeṣa*.

The second interpretation, that of Narain, refers to the opposition of *sāmānya* and *viśeṣa* as "notional or logical categories rather than ontological ones" (Narain 1976: 211). In my opinion, the conceptualist interpretation of the Vaiśeṣika universals contradicts the realistic character of its doctrine as shown below. However, if we accept Halbfass's interpretation, what is then the sense of the *VS* (1.2.5) in his translation

---

20. *dravyatvaṁ guṇatvaṁ karmatvaṁ ca sāmānyāni viśeṣāśca* ॥ — *VSC*, *VSŚ*, 1.2.5.

(quoted above)? Taking into account the *VS* quest for economy, this repetition seems to be superfluous. And moreover, there arises another question as to the sense of "specific factors" — are they specific universals or ultimate particularities? Neither is acceptable.

If universals really depend upon cognition they should exist primarily in cognition. But such an interpretation contradicts not merely the tradition of commentaries, but also the *sūtra*s which follow (already discussed), as well as the two *sūtra*s from the Book 8, where it is said that it is cognition which depends on universals.

We will begin with *VSC*, 8.6 and then return to *VSC*, 8.5.

8.6. "[The cognition] with regard to substances, qualities and motions depends on *sāmānyaviśeṣa*."[21] Candrānanda explains that with reference to substances, qualities and motions [taken together] the cognition depends on the contact between the substance-support (of qualities and motions) and the organ of sense, as well as on the universal of existence; [if we take substances, qualities and motions separately] it depends on the specific universals "substantiality," etc. As a result of these two acts of cognition we have two ideas, expressed in two words: "existent" (whose meaning is existence — *sattā*) and "substance" (its meaning is substantiality). In this *sūtra*, *sāmānya* — is *sattā*, *viśeṣa* are specific universals in the same way as "substantiality."[22]

In the previous *sūtra*, 8.5. *sāmānyaviśeṣesu sāmānyaviśeṣābhāvāt tata eva jñānam*, *sāmānya* means that all the universals

21. *sāmānyaviśeṣāpekṣaṁ dravyaguṇakarmasu* ॥ — *VSC*, 8.6.

22. *dravyaguṇakarmasu dravyendriyasannikarṣāt sāmānyācca sattādeḥ sāmānyaviśeṣācca dravyatvādeḥ sat iti dravyam ityādi ca jñānam utpadyate. iha sūtre sāmānyaṁ sattā viśeṣā dravyatvādayaḥ, pūrvasūtre 'nyathā* ॥ — *VSC*, 63.

beginning from the *sattā*, and *viśeṣa* — only the *antyaviśeṣa* (the ultimate particularities). And my translation of this *sūtra* is as follows: "The cognition with regard to universals and ultimate particulars is based on them as such [because it is not based on their] universals or ultimate particulars." It is again an application of the anti-reflexive rule (qualities do not possess other qualities, etc.) in order to prevent a regression *ad infinitum*. If my understanding is correct, these *sūtra*s could be treated as a confirmation of the objective existence of universals as well as of ultimate particularities.

Thus, we have two kinds of opposition between *sāmānya* and *viśeṣa*. First, the opposition of the supreme or the highest universal *sattā* and the ultimate particulars, or *antyaviśeṣa*; second, the opposition of the notions produced by the mental operations of generalization and differentiation or inclusion and exclusion (*anuvṛtti-vyāvṛtti*). Taking this into account, I propose a new translation of the sequence of the *sūtra*s beginning from *VSC* (1.2.3).

As a particle *iti* often marks a quotation (of some word usage or of notion), I translate this *sūtra* (*sāmānyaḥ viśeṣa iti budhyapekṣam*) as follows: "[The judgements] "[this] is a general (common) factor, [this] is a specific factor depend on correlative cognition." I propose to understand this *sūtra* in the light of Patañjali's discussion (*Mbh.* to *Pan.* 1.1.66-67) in which he argues that the definition of what is *sāmānya* and what is *viśeṣa* depends either on the intention of the speaker or on the property of the object in its relation to another object (like father and son — one and the same person may be a father to one person as well as a son to another). Something in an individual thing may be common to the other things of the same class (a cow with regard to other cows) and the same common feature may be specific in regard to the individuals of another class (cow as compared to horse). The question here is not about a universal and the speaker's intention to express it either as a common or a specific factor, as in Halbfass's translation (and in Patañjali's first case), but about the individual thing understood in comparison with other individual thing (the *apekṣabuddhi* is close to Patañjali's second case — grasping the object in its relation to another object). This *sūtra* sounds to me as a formulation of a general rule concerning particular things (substances, qualities and motions). Further on, the *VS* examine three instances of its application: the highest universal, the lower universals and the ultimate particularities:

1.2.4. "[The universal] of existence is a purely general (common) factor." That means that in the process of cognition concerning individual things (substances, qualities and motions) the *sattā* presents a factor conductive to assimilation only.

1.2.5. "Substanceness, qualityness and motionness are general as well as specific factors."

The specific universals mentioned in this *sūtra* form the bases of both — assimilation and differentiation. Owing to them our relational cognition (*apekṣabuddhi*) defines a particular substance, quality or motion in words (*śabda*) and notions (*pratyaya*). In other terms, the sense of the words designating the individuals of these categories are the specific universals.

1.2.6. "[This rule applies to all the *viśeṣa*] except for the ultimate particularities."[23] This double sense of *viśeṣa* as both general and specific factors which occurs while our *apekṣabuddhi* produces cognitive acts both of inclusion and exclusion at once, is not valid for the ultimate particularities. That means that in no circumstances could the latter be a factor of assimilation.

23. *anyatrāntyebhyo viśeṣebhyaḥ* ॥ *VSC*, 1.2.6.

And with that we return to the *sūtra* from which we started our inquiry.

1.2.7. "[The universal of] existence is that which produces [the idea or notion] "existent" with regard to substances, qualities, and motions."

It may mean that the sense of the word *sat* is the universal of *sattā*. Perhaps, it is the Vaiśeṣika answer to the famous Patañjali's question about the meaning of words. However that may be, I can suggest a reason why the *sattā* applies only to *dravya*, *guṇa* and *karman* — the first three Vaiśeṣika categories, but not to *sāmānya*, *viśeṣa* and *samavāya*. If we regard *sattā* as a universal, we must agree that it cannot reside in or embrace other universals (like a big *matryoshka* with the smaller ones inside), it also cannot reside in the ultimate particularities, or in the inherence — all these possibilities will lead to the *anavasthā*.

Thus, we get a preliminary outline of the theory of universals which will be later developed by Candramatī, Praśastapāda, Vyomaśiva, Śrīdhara, Udayana and others. The *VS* as compared with *Praśastapādabhāṣya*, do not explicitly talk about the eternity of universals, do not call them *padārtha*s, do not divide them into higher and lower (*para-apara*) sub-varieties, do not mention their connection with *anuvṛtti* and *vyāvṛtti* — cognitive acts of inclusion or exclusion. What we find here is a distinction between three kinds of things: the higher universal of existence, the specific universals, and the ultimate particularities. As the attitude of the *VS* towards the number of the *padārtha*s is not very clear, there are two different versions of the system of categories — that of Candramatī and that of Praśastapāda. In my opinion, Candramatī is more faithful to the *VS* triple division mentioned above because he has three categories: *sāmānya* by which he understands the highest universal only, *antyaviśeṣa* — the ultimate particularities only. As for the specific universals, they constitute their own category — that of *sāmānyaviśeṣa*. Praśastapāda includes *sāmānyaviśeṣa* into the category of *sāmānya* and thus creates a certain ambiguity in his systematization of categories. The category of *sāmānya* is not a self-sufficient one, because the idea of specificity (*viśeṣa*) of the *sāmānyaviśeṣa* (lower universals) could not be explained in its own terms, we should resort to the help of *viśeṣa*, but the category of *viśeṣa* contains only the ultimate particularities. Thus, the two categories are not symmetrical as they are logically supposed to be. That is why it is important to return to the *VS* for a further investigation of its conception of universals.

The questions raised by Halbfass (he was a real virtuoso of problematization) present a challenge to the students of universals. Let us recall some of them. "Can we take it for granted that the category of universal (*sāmānya*) was established prior to the conception of "reality" or of "existence" as one of its instances? What is the ontological status of universals (including *bhāva/sattā*), particularities, and inherence? What qualifies them as "different objects (*arthāntara*) and as additional world constituents? In what sense can they be co-ordinated with the substances, qualities, and motions? In what sense can they be said to "be there" (Halbfass 1992: 142-43).

Whatever the historical order of origin with regard to universals, the universal of being and the category of universal may have been, purely logical considerations suggest that the introduction of the universal of existence is possible if there is already a concept or the idea of universals in the scholastic sense which, in its turn, is connected with ascribing to them an independent ontological status (*ante rem*). If, according to the *VS*, *dravya*, *guṇa* and *karman* are *artha* (objects), or world constituents (in Halbfass's terms), the universals are another kind of object (*arthāntara*) that is a different kind of world constituents and the latter is tantamount to the postulation or conceptualization of them as *padārtha*s — the categories. Thus, we may talk about the conceptualization of universals in the scholastic sense only in the case of their inclusion into the list of *padārtha*s or the list containing the kinds of world constituents. Even if the *VS* in Candrānanda's version do not call universals *padārtha*s, this must somehow be implied in calling them *arthāntara*.

Nevertheless, we must acknowledge that the arising of the Vaiśeṣika doctrine of universals would not be possible without the Vyākaraṇa's "preparations," namely without the discussion between Vyāḍī and Vājapyāyāna about the meaning of the word. First of all, it were the grammarians who made a distinction between individual, or particular objects, on the one hand, and, on the other hand, something thanks to which can be extracted from them an information that might be helpful in understanding the other objects, that is something common, that can be found in different cognitions. This distinction between the individual and the general was the most important premise of the ontological conception of universals.

The second premise consists in the idea expressed by Patañjali that *ākṛti* (class property) as compared with individual thing (*dravya*) is permanent (*nitya*) and its permanence is due to its *tattva* — essence — which does not disappear.[24] This permanence is not yet the ontological eternity, but it is something which may be ontologized in philosophical reflection.

---

24. *VMbh*, 1.30-32

The third important brick laid by the grammarians in the foundation of the Vaiśeṣika universals was the idea of singularity of the generic form as opposed to the plurality of individual things. By accepting this idea, the grammarians faced a problem formulated by the follower of Vyāḍī (*dravyavādin*): if there is only one generic form how could it inhere in different individuals? For one man could not be present simultaneously in different places (cf. the discussion in the commentary to *Pan.* 1.2.64). In response, the follower of Vājapyāyāna (*ākṛtivādin*) proposes a model of Indra inhering in everyone of his images. It is namely this very model which was used by the Vaiśeṣikas in their theory of universals.

As for the position of Patañjali himself towards the discussion between *ākṛtivādin* and *dravyavādin*, he formulates it under *Pan.*, 1.2.58. He argues that a generic term denotes both a substance and a class property and this denotation depends upon the speaker's intention. In the Vaiśeṣika, these denotations are ontologized by becoming the different entities: a class property becomes a universal which is related to the individual thing with the help of *samavāya*, or inherence. But at the same time, in the process of cognition, this universal may not only assimilate, but also differentiate (*anuvṛtti*, *vyāvṛtti*). In that way, the Vaiśeṣika developed the ideas that were already postulated by the grammatical tradition. I mean above all the commentary of PatañJali to *Pan.*, 2.1.1 where he evokes two points of view on the semantic connection : Semantic connection means (either) differentiation or relation"[25] — "differentiation" of one sense of the word and exclusion of all the others (*bheda*), and relation or "integration [of the different senses in one word meaning] (*saṁsarga*)."[26]

25. *sāmaṛthyaṁ nāma bheda saṁsargo vā* ॥ — *VMbh* I : 364 (25).

26. If we take a compound such as *rājapuruṣa* "king's man," the word "king's," taken separately, may refer to any possession of the →

Though the continuity between Vyākaraṇa and Nyāya is much more evident, we should not disregard the fact that Vaiśeṣika may also be considered — in certain regards — as a successor of the grammatical tradition.

Abbreviations

VSC — *Vaiśeṣikasūtras of Kaṇāda with the Commentary of Candrānanda*, ed. Muni Śrī Jambuvijayaji, GOS 136, Baroda: Oriental Institute, 1961.

VSŚ — *Vaiśeṣikasūtras of Kaṇāda with the commentary of Śaṁkara Miśra and Extracts from the Gloss of Janārāyana. Together with Notes from the Commentary of Candrakānta and an Introduction by the Translator*, Sanskrit Text and English Translation of Nandalal Sinha, SBH VI, Allahabad: Indian Press, 1911 (reprint Delhi: S.N. Publications, 1986).

PBh — *Word Index to the Praśastapādabhāṣya, A Complete Word Index to the Printed Editions of the Praśastapāda*, ed. J. Bronkhorst and Yves Ramseier, Delhi: Motilal Banarsidass, 1994).

VMbh — *Vyākaraṇa-Mahābhāṣya of Patañjali*, ed. F. Kielhorn, vol. I, Bombay, 1880.

References

Filliozat, Pierre-Sylvain, 1975, *Le Mahābhāṣya de Patañjali avec le Pradīpa de Kayaṭa et l'Uddyoṭa de Nāgeṣa*, Adhyāya 1, Pāda 1, āhnika 1-4. Traduction par P. Filliozat, Publications de l'Institut Francais d'Indologie, Pondichery.

———, 1978, *Le Mahābhāṣya de Patañjali avec le Pradīpa de Kayaṭa et l'Uddyoṭa de Nāgeṣa*, Adhyāya 1, Pāda 1, āhnika 8-9. Traduction par P. Filliozat, Publications de l'Institut Francais d'Indologie, Pondichery.

king, as well as the word a "man" may imply any master. When we say : "bring the king's man," the word "man" keeps the king away from other owners," and the word "man" "keeps the king away from other things owned" (Ibid., I : 364-65, Translation of S.D. Joshi).

——, 1980, *Le Mahābhāṣya de Patañjali avec le Pradīpa de Kayaṭa et l'Uddyoṭa de Nāgeṣa*, Adhyāya 1, Pāda 2, Traduction par P. Filliozat, Publicationsde l'Institut Francais d'Indologie, Pondichery.

Halbfass, Wilhelm, 1992, *On Being and What There Is, Classical Vaiśeṣika and the History of Indian Ontology*, Albany: SUNY Press.

Gajendragadkar, Veena, 1988, *Kaṇāda's Doctrine of the Padārthas, i.e. Categories*, (ŚGDOS 49) Delhi: Śri Satguru Publications.

Narain, Harsh, 1976, Narain, *Evolution of the Nyāya-Vaiśeṣika Categoriology, vol. I, Early Nyāya-Vaiśeṣika*, Categoriology, Varanasi, Bharati Prakashan.

Nozawa, Masanobu, 1994, "On the Vaiśeṣikasūtra 1.2.3," *AS/EA*, XLVIII 2: 833-45.

Potter, Karl, 1977, *Encyclopedia of Indian Philosophies*, vol. 2. *The Tradition of Nyāya-Vaiśeṣika up to Gaṅgeśa*, Princeton University Press.

Scharf, Peter, 1996, *The Denotation of Generic Terms in Ancient Indian Philosophy: Grammar, Nyāya, and Mīmāṁsā*, American Philosophical Society, Philadelphia.

3

The Ego-principle (Ahaṁkāra) as a Key Concept in the Sāṁkhyakārikā*

Michel Hulin

Every time we try to understand a highly paradoxical system like Sāṁkhya, that is apparently teeming with obscurities and contradictions of all kinds, the temptation is great, almost irresistible, to ascribe its obvious inconsistencies to the external circumstances of its formation. Precisely in the case of Sāṁkhya, we know all too well how intricate and even "chaotic" its "pre-history" may have been. Nethertheless, this type of purely historical explanation runs the danger of reducing the doctrine to a hopeless mixture of fundamentally heterogeneous elements. On the other hand, a strictly philosophical interpretation runs the opposite danger of dogmatically and arbitrarily reading into the text the interpreter's own views. However, there is perhaps a third way: that is trying to exhaust every possibility of interpreting a system from inside, in terms of its own immanent logic, and only after that turning to the available historical data in order to somehow account for the remaining irreducible inconsistencies. That's the way we are

---

* Originally published as "Reinterpreting ahaṁkāra as a possible way of solving the riddle of Sāṁkhya metaphysics" in *Asiatische Studien*, LIII 3, 1999.

going to follow here while tackling the classical problem of the so-called ambiguity of *tattvas* in the *Sāṁkhyakārikā*: are they, all things considered, psychological or cosmic in themselves? Our approach is rather unorthodox and may even appear exceedingly speculative at places, but it's a tentative one, that has no claim whatsoever to final certainty. What I would like to suggest is that classical Sāṁkhya should not be considered as "dead stuff," a matter of mere scholarly knowledge, but that it still makes sense to draw some intellectual and spiritual inspiration from it.

In this context, I would like first to mention briefly the position upheld by Rodney J. Parrot (1986) in his article "The Problem of Sāṁkhya *tattvas*."[1] Focusing on *kārikās* 22 to 24 which describe the emergence first of *buddhi*, then of *ahaṁkāra* out of it, and finally of the immediate products of *ahaṁkāra*, he rightly points out the impossibility of interpreting those entities — "judgement" and "ego-feeling" in his translation — either as personal or as cosmic. In the first case, that would lead to some sort of subjective idealism, clearly incompatible with the Sāṁkhya conception of Nature (*prakṛti*) as one. In the second case, we would have to assume some sort of cosmic or divine understanding and ego-feeling encompassing the multitude of the individual ones. Now, this again appears incompatible with the famous "atheism" of classical Sāṁkhya (as opposed to the so-called "epic Sāṁkhya" that is to be found in the *Bhagavad-Gītā* as well as in various Purāṇas).

Parrot's own solution boils down to admit that from k. 22 onwards (up to k. 62) reality is no more being described as it is in itself but from the point of view of the bounded "spirit" (*puruṣa*) who wrongly identifies himself with nature and its evolutes. Only that false identification will give birth to the

1. *Journal of Indian Philosophy*, 14, 1986, pp. 55-77.

human, psychological *buddhi* and *ahaṁkāra*: the latter ones should not be considered as genuine *tattva*s, like their cosmic counterparts, but as mere phenomena, possessing only so-called "experiential" reality. In this way, the otherwise blatant contradiction between the psychological and the cosmic aspects of these *tattva*s is bound to completely vanish.

Now, the trouble with Parrot's solution, on the one hand, is that the supposed shift of attitude from k. 22 onwards is just being read into the text, with no support either from the *kārikā*s themselves or from their commentaries. On the other hand, it leads to the assumption of such strange entities as "cosmic knowing" for *buddhi* (not to confound with any kind of "cosmic intellect" inasmuch as there is still no person at that stage) and "cosmic I-maker" for *ahaṁkāra*. As for the corresponding mental organs in men and other limited creatures, they would appear, along with their own functions, only "later," as the bound *puruṣa* start identifying themselves with those cosmic or suprapersonal *tattva*s in the way of "I am the *buddhi* and — oddly enough — "I am the I-maker." We would call this explaining *obscurum per obscurius* or cutting the Gordian knot instead of patiently trying to undo it.

So, we are going to make an attempt to steer some middle course between a purely philosophical and dogmatic interpretation and a purely historical one. In particular, we are going to suggest that that famous "ambiguity" should not be explained away at every cost, as it is deeply rooted, in fact, in the very foundations of classical Sāṁkhya.

First of all, we have to question that all too "natural" opposition between subjectivity and objectivity. It rests, of course, on the fundamental duality of *puruṣa* and *prakṛti*, so that our texts could in no way ignore or bypass it. However, the very context in which they introduce it sheds by itself some light on the scope and meaning of the duality within the Sāṁkhya system. Actually, we never come across any *direct* justification of it. It is being rather presupposed as the foremost condition of possibility of both *bhukti* (everyday experience) and *mukti* (final emancipation).[2] Here, indeed, the *puruṣa-prakṛti* polarity does not provide any real basis, because experience, as well as its cessation, requires sentient, individual beings, constantly related to their surroundings through organs of perception and action. Now, organs (*indriya*) — unlike mere instruments — can be conceived only as the private property of some individual living being who unequivocally distinguishes between "myself" and "not myself." Consequently, according to classical Sāṁkhya, such splitting up will take place not at the level of *buddhi* — which is clearly working in co-operation with the *manas* and the other *indriyas* — but at the level of *ahaṁkāra*. The *buddhi,* in spite of its being the first evolute of *prakṛti,* cannot really discharge its function before the appearance of *ahaṁkāra*, because, at this stage, it has no external world at its disposal to connect the (moreover only potential) subject to it. Only *ahaṁkāra* provides the basis for the subject-object relationship insofar as it gives birth (as *vaikṛta/bhūtādi*) to both the "subjective" and "objective" series (*manas-indriya* versus *tanmātra-mahābhūta*).[3] So, in a way, *ahaṁkāra* must precede *buddhi.*

The impossibility for *ahaṁkāra* to fit into the *buddhi-manas-indriya* sequence follows from a priori as well as from a posteriori arguments. On the one hand, an "intellect" makes sense only as belonging to some particular person. Now, at the very stage of creation, in which *buddhi* is supposed to come to light directly out of *prakṛti,* there is no room, in the general

2. See, for instance, k. 21.

3. See k. 24 : *tasmād dvividhaḥ pravartate sargaḥ* et k. 25.

frame of the system, for any kind of person, human or divine. On the other hand, a close examination of the special function of *ahaṁkāra,* called *abhimāna,* clearly shows its disparity from the specific functions of *manas* and *buddhi* (respectively *saṁkalpa* and *adhyavasāya*). On the basis of its etymology and of its use in common parlance *abhimāna* could be technically defined as an unduly extension (*abhi-*) of the I-notion to entities basically foreign to it and better designable as "that" (*tat*). At the psychological level it means something like "high opinion of oneself, self-conceit" (Monier-Williams).

Now, k. 30 and its commentaries describe the way the three internal organs are co-operating to produce a reliable knowledge of the external world as well as adequate answers to the various challenges that may arise from it. The function of *manas,* as an organ of perception, consists in bringing together (*saṁ-kḷp*) the various sense-data (visual, auditory and so on). As an organ of action, it co-ordinates (again *saṁ-kḷp*) the operations of the specialized *karmendriyas*: speech, locomotion and so on. As for the *buddhi,* it may also be considered as an organ of both knowledge and action, but at a higher level than *manas*: mental apprehension, ascertainment, judgement, resolution. Now, it seems that there is no real room for *abhimāna* in its proper meaning within the frame of that construction. This becomes evident from the commentaries of both Vācaspati Miśra and Gauḍapāda[4] on that part of k. 30 which deals with the "successive" (*kramaśaś*) functioning of the three organs. Vācaspati's commentary runs as follows: ". . . in dim light, a person has at first only a vague perception of a certain object; then, fixing his mind (*manas*) intently on it, he observes that it is a robber with his drawn bow and arrow levelled at him, then follows the self-consciousness

4. Unfortunately enough, the relevant passage of the *Yuktidīpikā* is missing.

(*abhimanyate*) that 'the robber is advancing against *me*'; and lastly follows the determination (*adhyavasāyati*) to run away from the place."[5] So here *abhimāna* — as represented by *abhimanyate* — is completely stripped of its usual pejorative connotation of "self-conceit": the traveller is surely right in considering the robber as an immediate threat to his money and possibly to his very life! The same holds good for Vācaspati's commentary on k. 36 where the forwarding of the sense-data to the *puruṣa* is being compared with the process of tax-collecting in ancient India for the benefit of the Royal Treasury.[6] Here the senses are equated to the heads of families in a village, the *manas* to a "village officer" (*grāmādhyakṣa*), the *ahaṁkāra* to a "District Governor" (*viṣayādhyakṣa*), the *buddhi* to the "Governor of the Country" (*sarvādhyakṣa*) and the *puruṣa* to the king. Here again *ahaṁkāra* fits gently into the sequence but at the cost of a complete loss of its original meaning: the "District Governor," as a matter of fact, is satisfied with "taking personal cognisance" (*abhimatya*) of the collected taxes and transmitting them to "the Governor of the country!"

That same awkwardness is still more perceptible in Gauḍapāda's commentary on k. 30 : "Thus, a person going along a road perceives an object at a distance, and is in doubt whether it is a post or a man: he then sees some characteristic mark, like a bird perching over it, and then in his mind . . . (*manas*), full of doubt, arises the determining judgement (*buddhi*) that it is a post, and the the ego (*ahaṁkāra*) approves: 'Well, it's certainly a post' (*ataḥ ahaṁkāraś ca niścayārthaḥ sthānur eveti*).[7]" Obviously, Gauḍapāda does not know what to do

5. *The Tattva-Kaumudī*, tr. Ganganath Jha, Poona Oriental Series 10, 1965, p. 106.

6. *The Tattva-Kaumudī*, op. cit., p. 116.

7. *The Sāṁkhyakārikā of Īśvarakṛṣṇa with the commentary of Gauḍapāda*, tr. by T.G. Mainkar, 2nd edn., Oriental Book Agency, Poona, 1972, p. 89.

with *ahaṁkāra*. That is why he takes it out of its "normal" place — between *buddhi* and *manas* — and reduces its role to a mere reiteration of the *buddhi*'s judgement.

So, *ahaṁkāra* does not seem to have any real utility in the field of perception and action. That leads us to suspect it of not being a genuine element of the psychomental structure of man, perhaps not even a *tattva* quite like others.[8] A possible clue to what *ahaṁkāra* may really stand for lies in k. 64, the only one to describe "from the inside" how liberation occurs in the wake of the crucial discrimination of *puruṣa* and *prakṛti*: "Thus, from the study (or analysis) of the priciples, the knowledge arises: I am not, nothing belongs to me. I do not exist," and this knowledge is complete because it is free from error, pure and solitary (*evaṁ tattvābhyāsān nāsmina me nāham ity apariśeṣam* । *aviparyayād viśuddhaṁ kevalam utpadyate jñānam* ॥).[9] It becomes evident, here, that a person may get access to the state of liberation only through the "implosion" of his or her *ahaṁkāra*. Once *ahaṁkāra* dissolves, as a direct result of

---

8. Admittedly, *ahaṁkāra* is considered everywhere in the texts of classical Sāṁkhya as immediately derived from *buddhi*. However, there are some stray indications that the Sāṁkhya thinkers themselves did not feel quite comfortable with such a sequence. In the *Yuktidīpikā* on k. 29, for instance, we come across a *pūrvapakṣa* which states that *ahaṁkāra* should be mentioned first at place. It leans on "some *śāstra*" (untraced) which reads: "What (form of) consciousness enters the child while it's lying inside the mother's womb? The consciousness: "I am," which pertains to the great self" (*kā nu bhoḥ saṁjñā matur udare avasthitaṁ praty abhiniviśata iti? asmīty eṣā māhātmī saṁvid iti*), The *Yuktidīpikā*, ed. and tr., Shiv Kumar and D.N. Bhargava, Eastern Book Linkers, Delhi, 1992, vol. 2, p. 227.

9. Tr. G.J. Larson, *Classical Sāṁkhya*, Motilal Banarsidass, Delhi, 1969, p. 279.

discrimination, the whole "subtle body," that is the central part of the *tattva*-structure, is bound to collapse (*nivartate*).[10] That would not be the case if liberation were equivalent to some kind of "private" *pralaya*. Then, the resorption would start from the last evolutes, that is the *mahābhūta*, and from there spread to the subtle elements, the senses and the *manas*, before reaching *ahaṁkāra* and finally *buddhi*.[11] In the same way, any isolated dissolution of *manas* as well as of *buddhi* would have only empirical consequences, like absent-mindedness, dullness, madness, etc. Let us conclude that the word *ahaṁkāra* stands here for something transcendental: neither a mundane reality nor an organ of thought, like *manas* or *buddhi*. Its constant connection with *abhimāna* ("self-overvaluation") invites us to consider it as the most concrete embodiment of that beginningless "ignorance" (*avidyā*) or "lack of discrimination" (*aviveka*) that the Sāṁkhya thinkers are never tired of exposing it as the fundamental cause of suffering and of transmigration. Now, *ahaṁkāra*, as the most direct expression of ignorance, will also be beginningless, and from there, precisely, we may gain some insight into the vexed question of the ambiguity of the intermediate *tattva*s.

We need first to come back to the mutual overlapping of the two fundamental principles as described in k. 20 : "Because of the proximity of the two — i.e. *prakṛti* and *puruṣa* — the unconscious one appears as characterized by consciousness. Similarly, the indifferent one appears as characterized by activity, because of the activities of the *guṇa*s:"[12]

---

10. See Gauḍapāda's commentary on k. 44, ed. Mainkar, p. 119.

11. See for instance Gauḍapāda's commentary on the word *liṅgam* in k. 10 : *layakāle pañca mahābhūtāni tanmātreṣu līyante tāni ekadaśendriyaiḥ sahāhaṁkāre sa ca buddhau sā ca pradhāne layam yātīti*, ed. Mainkar, p. 30.

12. G.J. Larson's translation (slightly modified), op. cit., p. 265.

tasmād tatsaṁyogād acetanaṁ cetanāvad iva liṅgam ।
guṇakartṛtve ca tathā bhavaty udāsīnaḥ ॥

This transcendental interplay makes room for an intermediate field, the reality of which is not ultimate but experiential and provisory. It enjoys neither absolute selfhood (the privilege of the *puruṣa*) nor complete objectivity (the privilege of the *prakṛti* or *avyakta*). At the same time, it provides a basis for the subject-object relationship insofar as it allows the *puruṣa* to appear as agent (*kartṛ*) and enjoyer (*bhoktṛ*).

In this context the genius of the Sāṁkhya thinkers was to resort to the notion of *guṇa* (whatever its origin in the history of thought) as a conceptual instrument to provide this intermediary, half-real field with a theoretical status and, first of all, with an intelligible internal structure. Actually, the *guṇa* can very easily be interpreted in terms of greater or lesser proximity (or remoteness from) the two basic *tattvas*. That is, the *sattva* imitates some of the most essential properties of the *puruṣa*, while the *tamas* shows a striking affinity to those of *prakṛti*. As for the *rajas*, we may look at it as reflecting the unsteady mutual balance of the two other *guṇas*. Moreover, according to k. 12, they "successively dominate, support, activate and interact with one another"[13] *anyonyābhibhāvāśra-yajananamithunavṛttayaś ca*. . . . The *guṇas* are mutually inseparable while at the same time in constant rivalry. None of them is ever in a position to completely supplant the two others.

That means we are bound to come across — according to the parallelism of macrocosm and microcosm which classical Sāṁkhya, like most philosophies of ancient India, seems to take for granted — the same overall re-partition of the *guṇas* in the living beings and in the universe. Everywhere, *sattva*

13. Ibid., p. 262.

will dominate "above," *rajas* "in the middle" and *tamas* "down below". Ontologically, it is obvious that the relative importance of *sattva* is constantly declining from *buddhi* downwards to the *mahābhūtas* (the reverse for *tamas*).[14] The same holds good for the cosmos, according to k. 54 and its commentaries where *sattva* is associated with gods and heavenly regions, *tamas* with the animal world and *rajas* with the human world.[15] In this way, the *guṇa* structure may be considered as the very foundation of a real ontological continuity extending throughout the whole field of the manifestation. This leads to various consequences, three of which have special relevance to our inquiry.

First, the *guṇas* can never be considered as purely subjective or as purely objective, neither as individual moods projected on to a "neutral" external reality nor as intrinsic properties of things, independently of their appreciation by human

---

14. It's interesting to remark in this context that *ahaṁkāra*, in spite of its coming just after *buddhi* in the hierarchy of *tattvas*, does not show any special affinity of that kind to *sattva*. More generally, it makes no sense to ascribe a more or less "sāttvic" or "tāmasic" *ahaṁkāra* to different species of living beings, or to different human individuals, or to the same individual at different moments of his or her spiritual evolution — one more proof that *ahaṁkāra* is not just an element of the psychic apparatus or a *tattva* among others in the manifested world.

15. Although the k. themselves insist on the essential unity of mankind (k. 53 : *mānuṣaś caikavidhaḥ*), there are clear marks in the Dharmaśāstra and Purāṇa literature of a somewhat different anthropology which tends to interpret — and justify — the social hierarchy of *varṇas* in terms of *guṇas* (for instance, the brāhmaṇas are more "sāttvic," the śūdras more "tāmasic," etc.). besides that, the constant association of mankind with *rajas*, the *guṇa* expressive of suffering, is well in accordance with the so-called "pessimism" of classical Sāṁkhya.

sensitivity. This becomes evident from Gauḍapāda's commentary on the expression *anyonya . . . vr̥ttayas'ca* in k. 12:

> Thus a beautiful and virtuous woman is a source of delight to all, and she herself is the cause of pain to her co-wives; and again, she herself produces delusion in the passionate — in this manner *sattva* leads to the manifestation of *rajas* and *tamas*. Again, just as a king, assiduous in protecting his people and punishing the wicked, produces pleasure in the good people, and pain and delusion in the wicked — in this manner *rajas* leads to the manifestation of *sattva* and *tamas*. Again, *tamas* leads to the manifestation of *sattva* and *rajas* by its own nature of covering : just as the (monsoon) clouds covering the sky cause happiness to the people (in general), urge the farmer to activity by their rain and produce delusion in the lovers in separation.[16]

The beautiful and virtuous woman, for instance, may be considered *in abstracto* as purely sāttvic. This is however impossible because of the necessary coexistence and mutual interplay of the three attributes inside every creature, animate or inanimate. Moreover, this sāttvic character of her will be acknowledged by those only who are not too much blinded by their own passions. On the other hand, the Sāṁkhya doctrine is not completely relativistic: this woman really deserves, as compared with some other women, to be called sāttvic. Those who consider her as such have some right to do so, even if some "reserves" of *rajas* and *tamas* are lying inside her, ready to allow her to appear in a different light to less neutral spectators.[17]

---

16. T.G. Mainkar's translation (slightly modified), op. cit., p. 40.

17. It would seem that one of the superiorities of *sattva* lies in the capacity it grants to recognize less reluctantly the real presence of *rajas, tamas,* and of itself, in other beings and in various →

Secondly, that same *guṇa*-structure has to be conceived as "cutting through" the different spheres of reality: physical, biological, psychical, intellectual, and even ethical or spiritual. *Tamas*, for instance, refers to heaviness and darkness (physical), vegetative life (biological), dullness (psychical), slow-wittedness (intellectual), delusion or infatuation (spiritual). *Sattva*, of course, will include the opposite qualities. In the same way, *rajas* will refer to restlessness (physical), drive or urge (biological), suffering and passion (psychical), ardour in controversy (intellectual), fierce asceticism (spiritual).[18] At the same time, this does not prevent the *guṇa*-structure from building the very foundation of their hierarchical order, with *tamas* predominating in the physical and biological realms, *rajas* in psychic life, *sattva* in spiritual life, etc. Such an ontological continuity, while ultimately compatible with the so-called Sāṁkhya doctrine, will eventually call for a complete reinterpretation of this dualism, so as to stress its difference from what is usually understood under that denomination in Western philosophy.

Thirdly, the subject-object relationship — as *jñāna, karma* and *bhoga* — is bound to appear as a particular case of a phenomenon of much wider extension : the interplay of *guṇa*s. Due to the overall extension of *prakṛti* and its evolutes, what is going on "inside" the subject, his concrete emotional and

→ situations. See, for instance, the *Yuktidīpikā*, 13 where the possibility of quasi-objective judgements is admitted in the case of "co-wives acting for a single purpose" (i.e. pleasing their common spouse), or of "the wives of noble men staying in their houses with their husbands," or to "farmers who have cut their crops," op. cit., p. 54.

18. This would call for English equivalents with the same wide semantic extension. For want of something better, we may resort, at a pinch, to "inertia" for *tamas*, "tension" for *rajas* and "lightness" for *sattva*.

cognitive life, is not fundamentally different from what is going on "outside" in the world. There is no unbridgeable gulf between internal or "psychological" events and external ones, the reason for that being that the very same *guṇa*s are at play on both sides. Spinoza's famous saying according to which "man is not an empire inside an empire" may be most fittingly applied to Sāṁkhya. It means that even the most sophisticated processes of thought, up to the threshold of crucial discrimination (*viveka*), have to be interpreted in terms of *guṇa*s co-operating with one another and reacting on one another. The *buddhi* in particular, is not really conscious by itself. It's just a very intricate complex of functions upon which the predominance of *sattva* (not exclusive of the two other *guṇa*s) confers the capacity of *imitating* the genuine consciousness that belongs to the sole *puruṣa*. There is no such thing as "thinking" as a purely immaterial process. Only the agility of the comparatively sāttvic *buddhi*, its almost complete lack of inertia (*tamas*!), incites us to confound its extremely fast but still temporal moves with the complete immobility (*akartṛtva*) of the *puruṣa*.

We may now perhaps begin to understand why the Sāṁkhya thinkers did not pay much attention to dilemmas that are crucial to us, like "is there only one cosmic *buddhi* or as many *buddhi*s as individual beings?," etc. Not that they were completely unaware of such questions: their admission of the periodic world dissolution (*pralaya*), for instance, does imply a certain consciousness of their relevance. However, oppositions like the one of general and particular (*samasta-vyasta*) were not fundamental for them. They were looking at them, at least implicitly, as belonging to that impure, only half-real sphere of experience that owes its existence to the transcendental confusion of *puruṣa* and *prakṛti*. We tried to characterize *ahaṁkāra* as the most direct designation of that confusion. Individual experience — both emotional and intellectual — makes sense only as long as *ahaṁkāra* prevails. Once it vanishes, in the wake of discrimination, there is no ground anymore to contrast the personal with the individual perspective. As for the "temporary" continuation of individual, psychic experience, the Sāṁkhya thinkers, quite understandably, were prepared to admit a certain degree of apparent contradiction within it, as a mark, so to say, of its ultimate lack of authenticity, also as a promise of its inevitable collapsing in a more or less remote future.

One of the main difficulties we are coming across while trying to understand classical Sāṁkhya lies in some hidden presuppositions of our own Western philosophical tradition. Among those presuppositions one of the most treacherous seems to go back at least to Descartes and his characterization of the soul or *res cogitans* as *dubitans, intelligens, affirmans, negans, volens, nolens, imaginans quoque et sentiens.*[19] While writing those lines Descartes was in no way conscious of making an intellectual choice or advocating some special philosophical thesis. He was just making explicit what he thought was everybody's implicit understanding of what the words *res cogitans* stand for. Nevertheless, starting from such premises, it's hardly possible, actually, to do justice to doctrines like Sāṁkhya (or Advaita for that matter) that tend to strip the spiritual principle of any concrete activity or sentiency, interpreting at the same time the whole psychological life on the lines of what is going on in the external world. To that extent, a fresh study of classical Sāṁkhya may still prove fruitful, especially in helping us to overcome — and firstly to become aware of — some of our most deep-rooted intellectual prejudices.

19. *Meditatio secunda* in F. Alquié (ed.), *Descartes, oeuvres philosophiques,* vol II, Garnier, Paris, 1967, p. 186.

4

The Difficult Task of Hitting the Mean

Aristotle's Mean (Mesotes) and Buddha's Middle Path (Majjhima Patipadā)

Victoria Lysenko

IF we want to compare Aristotle's doctrine with that of Buddhism, it would be more natural to consider, on the Buddhist side, such systematic thinkers as Nāgārjuna, Vasubandhu or Diṅṇāga, all of whom lived long after the Buddha. A comparison of Aristotle with the Buddha himself is a rather problematic enterprise, open to justified criticism. Aristotle, as a theoretical thinker, was interested in "what is," "existence," "being *qua* being" (*to ti en einai*). He inquired into those very matters which the Buddha, as a practical religious thinker, considered to be completely useless, futile, not leading to the *nirvāṇa*. Nevertheless, both of them — though incompatible with one another in their modes of thought — agreed at least on one very important and existential point: they clearly realized the extreme difficulty of attaining the ideal (ethical for Aristotle and religious for the Buddha). As far as this ideal is associated for both of them with the mean (or the middle), I will call it "the difficult task of attaining the mean." Both understood the mean as something more complex and more intricate then an equal distance from opposite ends, an arithmetical mean, or a mechanical equilibrium (equipoise). They presented the mean regarding human beings as a state (condition) which is never given a priori, established spontaneously, or found by pure chance, but, on the contrary, is the subject of a constantly renewable creative search. In these general, and, as one can see, quite antiseptic terms, I will try to work out some purposes common to both actors. Any specification of these in terms of particular tasks, goals, conceptions and teachings leads us to abandon the sphere of generalities and to speak about differences.

The first fundamental difference proceeds from the obvious fact that for Aristotle the mean was one of the crucially important ontological and metaphysical ideas, while for the Buddha it was rather a methodological principle exemplified in a system of methods aiming at the attaining of the *nirvāṇa* "the final blowing out" or "extinction" of sufferings. But in the time of the Buddha the middle was not yet a symbol of a certain ontological principle, which it had become later by the time of Nāgārjuna and his school, called Mādhyamaka, "The Middle."

Aristotle's Doctrine of the Mean

We can come across the idea of the mean in practically all the branches of Aristotle's doctrine, from ontology and metaphysics to ethics and politics. Aristotle argues that one can detect the mean "in everything continuous and divisible" if "there is excess and deficiency." And the basis of this continuity is a motion, "for motion is continuous and action is motion" (*Eud. Eth* II.3.1220b 21-35). In other words, the mean is characteristic of something continuous, existing in the form of arithmetical progression (from deficiency to excess), as well as of something dynamic, changeable and complex. In ethics, it is a virtue; in a syllogism — a middle term; in a state — a middle class; in time — a "now"; in man — a soul. But for every field of human activity mentioned, its mean is the only static and not developing point — a point of stable equilibrium in balancing between "excess" and "deficiency."

The intricacy of this term (the mean) is deepened by some symptomatic inconsistency between the principles of the discourse proclaimed by Aristotle himself and the real foundation of his philosophy. He repeatedly affirmed the principle of the excluded middle and the logical impossibility for something having contrary characteristics (for instance, *Metaphysics* 1011b 20). However, in his own reasoning about the Mind (*Nous*), the knowing subject and its object become one autonomous self-subsisting "existent," "what a thing is to be *per se*" (*to on en einai*), "final good" (*to ariston*), "actuality" (*entelechia*), "first mover" (*to proton kinoyn*) which is itself unmovable. All these notions presuppose a kind of closure, coincidence or concurrence between the contraries — a beginning (*arche*), or a cause (*aitia*), is at the same time an end, or a goal (*telos*). The latter is not only a result, a final moment of any development, it is initially present from the very beginning, or even before the beginning of things and processes. Thus, a goal, constituting a limit, presents itself both as the beginning and as the final cause and substance.[1] In other words, there is a hidden identity beneath the contraries.

1. "Limit means (1) the last point of each thing, i.e. the first point beyond which it is not possible to find any part, and the first point within which every part is; (2) the form, whatever it may be, of a spatial magnitude or of a thing that has magnitude; (3) the end of each thing (and of this nature is that towards which the movement and the action are, not that from which they are, though sometimes it is both, that from which and that to which →

The notion of the mean here comes to the fore — it is in the middle, that the beginning and the end, the cause and the goal come together. That is why ". . . in all our inquiries we are asking either whether there is a 'middle' or what the 'middle' is: for the 'middle' here is precisely the cause, and it is the cause that we seek in all our inquiries" (*Anal. Post.* 90a 10, tr. by G.R.G. Mure). According to J. van der Meulen, Aristotle's "mean, when it comes to the limit of penetration into a true nature of things, is the Mind in its purest form."[2]

Thus the mean is a structural and ontological notion — a kind of perfect, completely accomplished actual state (*entelechia*) through which "breathes" the Absolute and which, in its most perfect form, is the Absolute itself (*Nous, Theos*). The analysis of the ethical mean must be firmly based on these metaphysical principles.

In the *Nicomachean Ethics*, Aristotle defines a virtue as that which is "concerned with pleasures and pains and disposes us to do what is best, while vice disposes us to the contrary" (*Nic.* II 1104b 25, tr. by Hippocrates G. Apostle). But "to do the best" stands for keeping the mean in passions, pleasures and sufferings: ". . . according to its substance or the definition stating its essence, virtue is a mean . . ." (Ibid., 1107a 5). According to its definition, mesotes ("mean," "middle," "moderate") lies between two extremes: that of the "excess" (hyperbole) and that of the "deficiency" (elleipsis). Mesotes

---

→ the movement is, i.e. the final cause); (4) the substance of each thing, and the essence of each; for this is the limit of knowledge; and if of knowledge, of the object also. Evidently, therefore, 'limit' has as many senses as 'beginning,' and yet more; for the beginning is a limit, but not every limit is a beginning" (*Met.* 1022a 5-10 tr., W.D. Ross).

2. J. van der Meulen, *Aristoteles. Die Mitte in seinem Denken, Meisenheim*, 1951, c. 124-25.

itself may never be either in excess or in deficiency: "there is not an excess or a deficiency of moderation" (Ibid., 1107a 20-25). The mean is just the right amount of some action or feeling. At the same time, the mean is possible only when and where both extremes are present and a continuous transition between them (continuous in the sense of divisible, that is divisible at any point, as opposed to what is made up of distinct parts and hence only divisible between the parts).

As for the vices (Aristotle mentions malice, shamelessness, envy, and, of actions, adultery, theft, murder), no mean inheres in them as they are "bad in themselves," also "it is impossible therefore ever to go right in regard to them" (Ibid., 20-25, tr. by H. Rackham). However, there is no mean in temperance or in bravery, "because the mean is in a certain way an extreme (*meson kai ariston*)" (Ibid., 1107a 5, tr. by Hippocrates G. Apostle). It is important to stress that "extreme" here is something highly positive — that is why, I prefer rendering an *ariston* as "excellence," "perfection." In this way, one can emphasize more clearly the identity of the mean and the ideal state of things.

The virtues definable in terms of the middle between the extremes are characteristic of practical wisdom (*phronesis*), directing our feelings and behaviour in everyday life. Aristotle calls them ethical virtues — *ethike*. However, there is a higher mode of existence which distinguishes man from the other animals — a contemplative life, or life of intellectual contemplation (*bios theoretikos*), with its special kind of the virtues: the dianoethic (*dianoethikai*), and the most important of them — wisdom (*sophia*). These virtues, like the ethical virtues of temperance or bravery, are perfect regardless of the context in which they occur (or a progression between deficiency and excess) and thus "moderate" by their very nature.

Aristotle sorts the mean into two kinds: with regard to things, and with regard to us (*pros hemas*). In the first case, we can find a middle in a purely mechanical way: "By the mean of the thing I denote a point equally distant from either extreme, which is one and the same for everybody" (Ibid., 1106a 30, tr. by H. Rackham). As for the second case, there is no mean which would be "one and the same for everybody." So the virtue must be specified with regard to the individual capacities of men and according to their particular circumstances: ". . . by the mean relative to us, (I define) that amount which is neither too much nor too little, and this is not one and the same for everybody" (Ibid.). Anyone who wants to be virtuous must decide for himself or herself what is "good" or what is "bad" in any given situation. That is why: ". . . it is a hard task to be good, for it is hard to find the middle point in anything: for instance, not everybody can find the centre of a circle, but only someone who knows geometry. So also anybody can become angry — that is easy, and so it is to give and spend money; but to be angry with or give money to the right person, and to the right amount, and at the right time, and for the right purpose, and in the right way — this is not within everybody's power and is not easy; so that to do these things properly is rare, praiseworthy, and noble" (Ibid., 1109a 20). And earlier in the same work: ". . . error is multiform (for evil is a form of the unlimited, as in the old imagery, and good of the limited), whereas success is possible in one way only (which is why it is easy to fail and difficult to succeed — easy to miss the target and difficult to hit it); so this is another reason why excess and deficiency are a mark of vice, and observance of the mean a mark of virtue" (Ibid., 1106b 30).

"To hit the mean," "to find the middle," "to hit the target" — all these expressions evidence the active and even decisive role of the moral subject, its mental disposition and volition.

As Theodor Losev remarks, "the mean in virtue is not a choice between the preset contraries of good and bad, but it is a constant self-affirming of the living being as determining these contraries."[3] Aristotle associates ethical virtues (as contrary to the dianoethical) with volition (which is for him a choice — *kata proairesin* — *Ethic. Eud* 6, 1223a 18), rather than with knowledge. In other words, a mean is never known a priori, it is a dynamic, ever migrating and elusive point, so that to find and to "hit" it one must concentrate every volitional effort. If vice presupposes a motion either in the direction of excess or in the direction of deficiency, the mean, once attained, becomes for us something like the centre of a cyclone remaining unlovable and unchangeable, or the centre of gravity due to which a thing is stable (Aristotle argues that the earth is fixed because its centre coincides with the centre of the universe). The highest goal which is pursued for its own sake but not as a means of attaining any other goal, is the "utmost good" (*to ariston*), the "good in itself" (*tagaton*) and it is for Aristotle "an activity of soul according to virtue" — happiness (*eudaimonia*) consisting of reason or activity according to reason (*Nic. Eth.* 1099b 25-30). Concerning virtue, "with respect to the highest goal and to excellence, it is an extreme" (Ibid., 1107a 5). In this context, the extreme is also not an excess, but the highest point, the summit. Thus, as we can see, the circle is closed: the mean, from the point of view of the highest value (that of the *bios theoretikos*), tends to be the utmost good (*to ariston*), the symbol of plenitude and excellence, the highest self-sufficient goal. After attaining it, a man continues his activities (because a happiness manifests itself in activity), yet they are not directed to any outer end beyond intellectual contemplation.

---

3. A. Th. Losev, *History of Ancient Aesthetics, Aristotle and the Late Classics*, Moscow, Iskusstvo, 1975, c. 637 (in Russian).

The Buddha's Sermon on the Middle Path

Now let us turn to the Buddha's famous sermon about the Middle path:

> These two (dead) ends (*anta*), monks, should not be followed by one who has gone forth. Which two? That which is, among sense-pleasures, addiction to attractive sense-pleasures, low, of the villager, of the average man, not connected with the good; and that which is addiction to self-torment, ill, not connected with the good. Now, monks, there is a middle course, fully awakened by the Truthfinder, making for vision (knowledge of the truth), making for knowledge, which conducts to calming (of the passions), to super-knowledge (*abhijñā*), to awakening (*sambodhana*), to *nirvāṇa*.
>
> — Mahāvagga, 17, *The Book of the Discipline*, PTS, vol. IV, 1962, tr. I.B. Horner.

As for the difficulties of pursuing the middle path or the middle course, the texts of the Buddhist Pali canon, which we will take as our main authority in matters concerning the early Buddhist teaching, are very wordy about it while describing the *Dhamma* (Buddha's teaching, Truth). For in these texts, the middle path is sometimes directly identified with *Dhamma*. The formulaic description of the *Dhamma* as "profound, indiscernible, difficult to accomplish, good, perfect, inaccessible to reasoning, exquisite, accessible only to experts" refers as well to the middle path. In what does a middle path consist? In the Buddha's teaching it is a system of the eight practical rules (Eightfold Path): (1) right views — right understanding of the nature of existence in terms of the Four Noble Truths; (2) right intention — the resolve to practise the faith; (3) right speech — avoidance of falsehoods, slander, or abusive speech; (4) right action — abstention from taking life, stealing, and improper sexual behaviour; (5) right livelihood

— rejection of occupations not in keeping with Buddhist principles; (6) right effort — avoidance of bad and development of good mental states; (7) right mindfulness — awareness of the body, feelings, and thought; and (8) right concentration — meditation. The whole network of rules covers three main domains: moral behaviour (2, 3, 4), practice of meditation (7, 8) and practice of knowledge (1). The most important among them is the right understanding, or right view (*sammādiṭṭhi*). As for the rules of moral behaviour (*śīla*), the majority of them are common to almost all ascetic movements in India and contain nothing specially Buddhist. Though some meditational practices (*samādhi*) were also not of Buddhist origin, it is important to stress that they are at the centre of Buddha's teaching and his contribution to the religious life in India is mainly connected with them.

Thus the main difficulty lies not in choosing the only "right" mental disposition among many "wrong" ones, representing excess or deficiency in some respect ("right" or "wrong" they are not with regard to some moral principle, as we will see later), but while systematically practising yogic and meditation exercises to be in tune with the highest Buddhist goal, the elimination of egocentric attachments to the values of worldly existence (*saṁsāra*) and the attainment of enlightenment and the *nirvāṇa*.

While for Aristotle the ethical mean pertains mainly to a life in the polis, in society, among other fellow-citizens, — and his "extremes" are also in the sphere of socially determined human connections, for the Buddha the "extremes" (*anta*) belong to different spheres and no gradual or continuous transition between them is possible. The first "extreme" (of sensuous indulgence) concerns the sphere of worldly life (though some monks can still be subject to it), and the second is characteristic of the ascetic way of life, that is the life outside lay society and outside social connections (the ascetic communities have their proper forms of communication). So, the middle path could not be situated in between these two modes of life, social and religious. It is rather on the monastic path, for the Buddha seems to believe that the final release is possible only for monks.

In *Aṅguttara Nikāya*, the Buddha calls those who are attached to sensual pleasure "hardened sensualists" (*āgālha-gāllhā, kakkhallā, lobha-vasera*) and those attached to mortification, self-tormentors. The most important of Buddha's contribution to this highly important domain of religious life in ancient India is a certain detente in the religious struggle against the human body. If we treat Buddha's ideas about the middle path in terms of Aristotle's principles (virtue is virtue regarding some particular occasion or situation), we could call the situation in question — an attitude towards the human body. In temporal pleasures there is an excess, in acetic mortification a deficiency, of attention to the human body; both are vicious. The mean lies in an attitude that, according to the Buddha, makes the body an efficient instrument of spiritual life and that demands certain attention to its physical and physiological needs. The Buddha himself, as we remember, attained his enlightenment only after renouncing hard ascetic practices which had led him to complete physical exhaustion, and after having regained his health. He accepted it as an inevitable fact that, to accomplish spiritual progress, one needs a body which would be in a "working state," and for this reason one should always exercise control over all bodily needs.[4]

4. In the *Gaṇakamoggalānasutta*, he says to a monk named Gaṇaka Moggallāna: "Come you, monk, be moderate in eating; you →

While Aristotle acknowledges that sensual pleasures may have their mean in the form of prudence (*sophrosyne*), the mean between libertinism (*akolastos*) and insensibility (*analgesia*) (*Nic Eth.* 1117b 25-1118a 2), the Buddha completely extracts sensual pleasures from the sphere of "moderation." He regards all sensual pleasures as *kilesa, āsava* — these and like terms connote affliction, defilement, obstacles on the way to spiritual progress. The mean consists in their full neutralization (with the help of special meditative practices, for instance the practice of mindfulness — *satī*). No moderation is feasible here. Sensual pleasures do not admit of a "mean" because, to use Aristotle's expression, they are vicious "by their very nature."

In this respect, the ascetic way of life is different from the sensual life in which the mean is not only possible, but highly desirable. Thus, if the first extreme is a "pure" vice (in Aristotle's sense), the second is subject to different appreciations, depending on the situation.

In the *Devadahasutta*, the Buddha explains to Jaina monks what is for him "fruitful striving," "fruitful effort", ". . . a monk does not let his unmastered self to be mastered by anguish (*dukkha* — V.L.), and he does not cast out rightful happiness and is undefiled by this happiness." He compares an attitude of a monk towards pleasures (happiness) with the attitude of a man towards a woman he was once in love with: ". . . he may see her standing and laughing with another man

→ should take food reflecting carefully, not for fun, or indulgence or personal charm, or beautification, but taking just enough for maintaining this body and keeping it going, for keeping it unharmed, for furthering the Brahma-faring, with the thought: 'Thus will I crush out an old feeling, and I will not allow a new feeling to arise, and then there will be for me subsistence and blamelesness and abiding in comfort'" (*Majjhima Nikāya*, vol. III (2), L., PTS, 1959, tr. B. Horner).

. . . and grief, sorrow, suffering, lamentation and despair do not rise up (in him)." If that monk has eliminated these unpleasant states and has developed some equanimity, there may be a moment when he says to himself: "Dwelling as I please, unskilled states (*akusala dhamma* — V.L.) grow much, skilful states (*kusala dhamma* — V.L.) decline, but while striving against myself through anguish (*dukkhāya pana me attānam padahato*) unskilled states decline, skilled states grow much. . . . After a time he does not strive against his self through anguish. What is the reason for this? Monks, the purpose of that monk who might strive against his self through anguish is accomplished. . . . It is like a fetcher who heats and scorches a shaft between two firebrands, and when he has made it straight and serviceable, he no longer heats and scorches the shaft between the two firebrands to make it straight and serviceable . . . the purpose is accomplished" (*Majjhima Nikāya*, vol. II:222-28).

In his conversation with Sonna Kolivisa who has injured his feet during his ascetic exercises, the Buddha asks whether it is possible to play the lute if its strings are too taut or too slack. After Sonna's negative answer the Buddha asks: "When the strings of your lute were neither too taut, nor too slack but were keyed to an even pitch was your lute at that time tuneful and fit for playing?" Sonna certainly agrees. And applying this situation to ascetic efforts the Buddha summarises:

> Even so, Sonna, does too much output of energy conduce to restlessness, does too feeble energy conduce to slothfulness. Therefore, do you, Sonna, determine upon evenness (*samatam*) in energy and pierce the evenness of the faculties (*indriyānāṁ ca samataṁ pattivijja*) and reflect upon it.
>
> — *Mahāvagga*, V.1.15-16.

Here, the keyword for us is *samatānām*, or *sama*, *samatā* — "the same," "the like," "equal," "evenness" ("the same at the beginning, the same in the end, the same in the middle" — in this way the Buddhist texts characterize *Dhamma* (the Buddha's teaching).[5]

Thus, only that practice is fruitful and efficient which contributes to progress on the way to *nirvāṇa*. If a monk practising *samathā*, or elimination of the affects, has become calm to the point of slothfulness and obtuseness, a little bit of self-torture would do him good: it may brace him and pull him further to his final goal. So, under certain circumstances, the extreme of "self-mortification" is quite acceptable.

We can notice that the Buddha never suggests to cheer monks up with the contemplation of a beautiful woman or anything similar. The other extreme is, therefore, completely useless for salvation. The Buddha's attitude towards sensual pleasures is clearly expressed in *Mahādukkhakkhandhasutta*. He classifies five varieties of sensual knowledge: visual, auditory, olfactory, gustatory and tactile. The major part of this *sutta* is dedicated to a picturesque account of all sorts of miseries due to the attachment to these: affliction by the cold, heat, suffering from the touch of gadflies, mosquitoes, wind, sun, creeping things, dying of hunger and thirst.

Any worldly occupation, any craft, may lead a man to the loss of his fortune, to failure, and thus to suffering from the

---

5. We also find the identification of the mean with sameness or evenness in Aristotle: "Now of everything that is continuous and divisible, it is possible to take the larger part, or the smaller part, or an equal part, and these parts may be larger, smaller, and equal either with respect to the thing itself or relatively to us; the equal part being a mean between excess and deficiency" (*Nic. Eth* II 1106a 4).

fruitlessness of his efforts. Even in the case of success, a fortunate man will be afraid of his possessions and may as well lose them. The cause of all this is our attachment to sensual pleasures. It is for them that "kings dispute with kings, nobles dispute with nobles, brāhmaṇas dispute with brāhmaṇas, householders dispute with householders, a mother disputes with her son, a son disputes with her mother, a father disputes with his son, . . . a brother disputes with a brother, a brother disputes with a sister, . . . a friend disputes with a friend. Because of them, there are battles, wars, murders, thefts, punishments, tortures and so on."

In the same *sūtta*, we find a characteristic attitude towards a beautiful woman: "one might see the same lady after a time, eighty or ninety or hundred years old, aged, crooked as a rafter, bent, leaning on a stick, going along palsied, miserable, youth gone, teeth broken, hair thinned, skin wrinkled, stumbling along, the limbs discoloured" (*Majjhima Nikāya,* I. 184-190). Imagining a young beauty in this way, a man can eliminate his attachment to material form.

In this case, the Buddha has applied a tactic of introducing the antidote (*pratipakṣa*), which will be developed in detail in Theravāda Buddhism. Both attraction and aversion (*rāga-dveṣa*) are affects, defilements, but the aversion or disgust may become just the right dose of poison to serve as a good medicine. From the repugnance towards body elements (*Viśuddhimagga* recommends contemplating these elements in their most disgusting form, for instance, the hairs in food), as well as from contemplating the different stages of cadaveric decomposition there arises a soteriologically relevant property of *vairāgya* — a detachment, an indifferent attitude towards the material world.

The Buddha rejects sensual pleasures so radically primarily because of their capacity to produce attachment to something which is temporal and transient and thus could not serve either as a stable foundation for existence, or as a way to it. All negative sensations and emotions connected with pain and suffering have, in this respect, an important advantage: it is not so easy to become attached to them (except for cases of masochism, certainly unknown to the Buddha — to my knowledge he never speaks about pleasures in suffering). Moreover, they contribute to the disruption of these attachments. That is why we can use them for the benefit of our spiritual progress. The same holds good in respect to ascetic self-mortification practices; though detestable by their very nature, under certain circumstances they may be quite appropriate.

One example is from the *Vajjiyamahitasutta*. The Buddha explains to the householder *Vajjiyamahita* that his attitude towards ascetic practices is not a categorical one (*ekāntika*):

> Indeed, householder, I say not that all ascetic ways are to be pursued. I do not say all ascetic ways are not to be pursued. I say not that every undertaking, that every effort in training should be undertaken and made. Yet I do not say the opposite. I say not that every renunciation should be made, nor yet that it should not be made. . . . If in one practising austerities unprofitable states (*akusala dhamma* — V.L.) wax and profitable states (*kusala dhamma* — V.L.) wane, such austerity should not be practised, I declare. If in one undertaking the training . . . making an effort . . . making renunciation, unprofitable states wane and profitable states wax, such undertaking, or training, such making of effort, such making of renunciation should be made, I declare.
>
> — *Aṅguttara Nikāya*, V, 190-192, tr. F.L. Woodwart, *The Book of the Gradual Sayings*, PTS, L., 1955.

As we can clearly see, the Buddha's strategy consists of avoiding categorical and general statements. He judges all these practices strictly selectively, according to their capacity to contribute to or to impede the spiritual progress of a particular man in a particular situation. (The Buddha is often called *vibhājjavādin* — one who knows how to divide or analyse.) It is the best way to formulate the later Buddhist principle of *upāya kauśalya*, the skilful means of converting (people to Buddhism). The Buddhist way to emancipation is not one and the same for everybody. The Buddha accommodates it to the individual character of his followers, but his general strategy is to find in each a certain point of dynamic spiritual growth, through which one can "grow out" up to the *nirvāṇa*. The middle path is not a walk down a smooth and direct road with a measured tread; it is rather a manoeuvre across a minefield — one step does not ensure the success of those which follow. On the other hand, the middle path is not a stable equilibrium, settled once and forever, but a constant declination to one or the other side, aiming to fit the ever changing "disposition of forces." The most important thing here is not a point of equilibrium, but rather a point of growth. In this, in my opinion, lies the main difference between the "hard task of attaining the mean" for Aristotle and for the Buddha.

According to Aristotle, virtues and vices do not form constant properties of the soul, but they emerge only under certain circumstances ("at the right time, on the right occasion, towards the right people, for the right purpose and in the right manner" *Nic. Eth.* II, 1106b 20). For instance: "A man is temperate if he abstains from bodily pleasures and finds this abstinence itself enjoyable, profligate if he feels it irksome; he is brave if he faces danger with pleasure or at all events without pain, cowardly if he does so with pain" (Ibid., 1104b).

So, Aristotle, like the Buddha, applies a differential, situational analysis and in this sense we can also call him *vibhajjavādin*.

Nevertheless, he constantly insists on the self-sufficient character of the contemplative life (*biōs theoretikos*). The image of perfection and plenitude is for him a kind of circle (among the movements the most perfect is a circular one). Having reached the middle (the mean), a sage finds himself at the point of equilibrium, the point of realized actual being (*entelechia*) which is stable and unmovable like the centre of a cyclone. The Buddha, on the contrary, insists on the transient character of all the meditative techniques constituting the middle path. None of the good mental states which can be achieved by the Buddhist follower is self-sufficient or stable. For all the *dhammas* (mental states) are transient (*anicca*) and without any proper essence (*anatta*), whether they are "profitable" or "unprofitable."

In the *Mahānidānasutta*, the Buddha explains to Ananda what it means to be a released monk: ". . . when a monk attains these eight emancipations (*jhāna* — V.L.) in forward order, in reverse order, in forward and reverse order, when he attains them and emerges from them wherever he wants, however he wants, and for as long as he wants." Thus it is important not only to attain meditative state, even the highest one, but also to emerge from it, that is to be free from the attachment to it. However much you like it and feel good in it, it is nothing but a transient step which must be overcome, not a goal in itself. As for the goal, it lies beyond all normal human capacities, including reasoning and rational understanding: ". . . when through the ending of the mental fermentation he enters and remains in the fermentation-free release of awareness and release of discernment, having directly known it and accomplished it in the here and now, he is said to be a monk released in both ways." (*Dīgha Nikāya*, II.70, tr. by Thanissaro Bhikkhu). Thus, the resulting state is something beyond the other states of the middle path, beyond all varieties of saṁsāric existence (past, actual, or future), beyond the human condition as such. It transcends the contemplative soul (*to dianoeéticon*), intellect or mind (*Nous*) so dear to Aristotle. The *nirvāṇa* is a transpersonal state, quite the opposite of what a human being knows and feels in his or her human experience. We can say that the *nirvāṇa* is transcendent, whereas Aristotle's *to ariston* (*Nous, entelechia*, etc.) having relation to the foundation of human experience, is, in my opinion, transcendental.

The other difference, which results from this one, is a matter of the moral or rather of the ethical status of the mean. Aristotle tries to justify the mean in moral categories. The Buddha resorts not so much to moral as to pragmatic categories: his opposition *kusala-akusala*, advantageous (profitable) or disadvantageous (unprofitable), relates to the practical effect of approaching the *nirvāṇa*. In discussing moral practices proper (which constitute only the third part of the middle path), the Buddha accentuates not their "morality," but their practical efficiency.

The Buddha is often compared with the physician, but this comparison is justified only with regard to the means and not to the goal of his teaching. We can say that the individual defilement of the Buddhist adept conditions the character of the practices recommended to him in the same way as the character of illness determines the character of remedy recommended by a physician. However, for the Buddha well being and good health of a person are only a means for obtaining the transpersonal state, while for Aristotle they are a *sine qua non* for the moral perfection of the person (the ideal of *kalokagatia*).

I have already mentioned that the principle of the mean infuses the whole of Aristotle's doctrine. The same is true for the Buddha's as well. The mean for him is a support — in the most efficient mode of their functioning — not only of the behaviour, but also of emotional and intellectual activity, constantly renewed balance productive of spiritual progress, while the "extremes" are a pure waste of energy, a sort of entropy, binding a person to his or her *saṁsāra*, a circle of rebirth in the world of suffering. That is why, in his attitude towards the so-called "metaphysical questions" (the finiteness or infinity of the world, the existence or non-existence of the soul and so on) the Buddha never says categorically (*ekāntika*) either "no," or "yes." In polemics with other teachers or their followers he tries to budge them from their "extreme" (categorical) position, and for this purpose he points to the possibility of the opposite extreme. In other words, to arrive at the equilibrium he intentionally overloads the counter-weight. For instance, to sceptics he praises the advantages of dogmatic views, and to those who do not believe in post-mortem existence he describes the benefits of this belief: if it does not exist the believer may at least win the respect of social opinion, and if it really exists he wins a double prize — in this and in the other world; as for the sceptics they are defeated in both cases (*Appanaka Sutta, Majjhima Nikāya* I.403-404). In the Brāhmanical traditionalists, believers in the supreme *Brahman* and in possibility of their "union" with Him, he provokes hesitation by asking them whether they have seen this *Brahman*, or know somebody who has seen Him, and finally he compares the believer in *Brahman* with a man who tells everybody how he loves the most beautiful woman in this land whom he knows not and has not seen (*Tevijja Sutta, Dīgha Nikāya* XIII.19).

As for the "positive" statements made by the Buddha himself, all of them purport to offer a "moderate," "middle" decision to the problems to which other teachers seem to give too categorical, extreme interpretation. He applies the *catuṣkoṭika* scheme (*tetralemma*) which tends to prove that none of the "categorical" statements[6] is acceptable. In the *Acelasutta*, the crucial Buddhist doctrine of the dependent origination (*patticca samuppāda*) is presented as the middle way between eternalism (belief in the eternity of soul — *sassatavāda*) and annihilationism (*ucchedavāda* — belief that the soul is destroyed at the moment of death). Acela Kassapa, an ascetic, asks the Buddha whether a *dukkha* (suffering) is a result of actions of the person himself, or of somebody else. The Buddha answers that none of these suggestions hold good, for the *dukkha* results from *patticca samuppāda* (*Saṁyuta Nikāya* II.18-21).

As we have seen, under certain circumstances, when there is a need to create a counterweight to another "extreme," the middle disposition may coincide with the "extreme." For example, there is the "neutralization" of attachment to sensual pleasures with the help of aversion to the disgusting aspects of the dead body. In the same way, torpor is to be overcome by mental activity, and so on.

A certain "manipulation" of "extremes" in order to achieve perfection is also characteristic of Aristotle (see: *Nic. Eth.* 1109b 25), but "perfection" (*to ey*) is for him the same as "beauty" (*to kalon*). We cannot say the same in the case of the Buddha, for whom aesthetic contemplation was nothing but a source of attachment to the material world, and in that way, an obstacle to *nirvāṇa*. For the Buddhist follower is primarily a practitioner: he constantly tackles, that is, passes through the sieve of

6. (1) *A* is *P*, (2) *A* is not *P*, (3) *A* is *P* and *A* is not *P*, (4) *A* is neither *P*, nor no-*P*.

consciousness, all his mental states to eliminate those which have nothing to do with his progress to the final release (*nirvāṇa*).

The Buddha, like Aristotle, was sure that professional activity is not fit for a wise man: but for the Buddha it is because it is subject to sufferings, and for Aristotle it is due to the absence of leisure (*skhole*) and its character of being pursued not for its own sake but for other goals. On the other hand, a wise man in Aristotle's opinion is not a wandering ascetic with his basic needs, but anybody rich enough to have leisure for a contemplative life, though abstemious in his sensual desires.

However, it would be unfair to Aristotle to see him only as a purely unreligious, rational thinker, extraneous to any spiritual or religious quest. In the *Nicomachean Ethics* Aristotle ascribes to a sage an aspiration to overcome the human condition:

> Such a life as this however will be higher than the human level: not in virtue of his humanity will a man achieve it, but in virtue of something within him that is divine; and by as much as this something is superior to his composite nature, by so much is its activity superior to the exercise of the other forms of virtue. If then the intellect is something divine in comparison with man, so is the life of the intellect divine in comparison with human life. — *Nic. Eth.* X.1177b 30.

His Absolute, *Nous*, is at the same time God (*Theos*) — not a personal God interested in this world, but pure intelligence completely indifferent to world affairs (as is implied in the concept of the unmoved mover). Though the status of Aristotle's *Nous* remains relatively indeterminate, and in any case it cannot be interpreted either as entirely transcendental, or as transcendent, it is not just an accidental coincidence that this *Nous* serves as the basis for the Neoplatonism of Plotinus and Porphyry with its transcendent One and it is not by pure chance that Plotinian texts were translated into Arabic under the title: *The Theology of Aristotle.*

The Buddha's middle path also has not remained a merely pragmatic methodological principle. Its transformation into a metaphysical and philosophical doctrine achieved its full realization in the Madhyamaka, in which the contraries, *saṁsāra* and *nirvāṇa*, coincide, shaping the material world infiltrated by the spiritual essence ("Buddha's nature," "emancipation," "vacuity"), in the same manner as the material world of Aristotle is penetrated by "forms" or "images" (*eidos*) proceeding from the supreme Mind (*Nous*).

Thus, we can see that the notion of the mean in itself, presets a certain structure of reasoning, so that even such thinkers as Aristotle and the Buddha — otherwise different — show some symptomatic coincidences. If the mean is estimated as the highest value, we must have the "extremes" and some difficulties (whether of ethical, metaphysical, or religious character) in detecting it. Aristotle seems to think that, once attained, the mean remains intact, permitting a sage (ideal person) to lead entirely self-sufficient contemplative life (*bios theoretikos*). On the contrary, even after stepping on the Buddhist path, a monk continues to face the constant danger of losing it because none of the practices recommended by the Buddha is to be exercised on its own behalf. The highest goal, pursued for its own sake, the *nirvāṇa*, is another kind of experience — experience beyond the chain of causation productive of transmigrational experience, beyond the person as such.

5

Reinterpretations of Karman in Contemporary Western Societies

Michel Hulin

THE idea of souls transmigrating from body to body, through a long series of rebirths, has been among the earliest documented and most widespread beliefs of humankind.[1] But in the West, at least until very recently, it could not escape remaining rather marginal in the face of the uninterrupted domination of Christianity, whose innermost tendencies have consistently taken it in a quite different, if not opposite, direction.

Nowadays, however, various signs lead us to think that this state of things is in the process of changing, and with surprising speed. A whole series of polls or surveys, conducted at regular intervals throughout the last quarter of the twentieth century, especially in the English-speaking world, converge to highlight the fact that this belief in reincarnation has been gaining ground at lightning speed. In Great Britain, for instance, the belief would today be shared by over a quarter

1. One could become convinced of this, notably, by reading the masterly general survey which Helmuth Zander recently devoted to the subject: *Geschichte der Seelenwanderung in Europa, Alternative religiöse Traditionen von der Antike bis heute,* Primus Verlag, Darmstadt, 1999.

of the adult population (as compared with 5 per cent in 1974).[2] We must certainly guard against taking these quantitative data too literally. As the very idea of reincarnation can be interpreted in quite different ways, "believing" or "not believing" in it would necessarily embrace a wide range of shades of meaning which would remain in principle ungraspable by any questionnaires, given their relative lack of subtlety.

However, there is no doubt as to the general direction in which the collective paradigm is heading, all the more so since the results of these surveys are corroborated by a multiplicity of convergent clues — in the first place, by proliferation of a literature devoted to these issues and the success it has had with the public. Well-known individuals who in other epochs, fearing to be branded heretics or simply for fear of ridicule, would have kept these confidences private, do not hesitate nowadays to parade their previous lives. The media: radio, television, even the cinema (let us recall Bertolucci's *Little Buddha*) have also been eagerly taking up this theme.

Thus, at the beginning of the twenty-first century and at the very heart of the Western world, the idea of transmigration, while not yet mainstream, strictly speaking, is being taken seriously by an ever-increasing number of people. Are we simply witnessing a fad, something more or less superficial and ephemeral? Or is a much broader and deeper change of

---

2. H. Zander (p. 601) gives a chart summarizing the results of the most recent of these surveys for the main countries of western and eastern Europe as well as for the Americas. The average hovers around 25 per cent, with peaks above 30 per cent (Poland, Brazil). Also, in Québec, where 80 per cent of the population call themselves Catholic, a 1984 survey revealed that about 20 per cent of those surveyed held some sort of belief in reincarnation.

mentality taking place? We shall here suggest some tentative responses to this question.

At first sight, the most likely answer would be to see the phenomenon as simply a revival of one of the many metaphysical and religious themes originating in Buddhism and Brāhmanism. After all, already in antiquity, India was regarded as the land of transmigration (Skt. *saṁsāra*) *par excellence*. But can we really see this ideology of reincarnation which is becoming more and more widespread here, as a faithful copy or simple adaptation of the classical doctrine of *saṁsāra*, or does it rather emerge from a wholly different intention?

In traditional India, belief in successive rebirths is, so to speak, taken for granted. That is to say that it never appears to be the outcome of any specific thought process. It is the very opposite of a conscious, deliberate stand which would be taken by this or that person individually. People are raised in this belief and are imbued with it from a young age, so much so that the very idea of questioning it is very likely to not even occur to them during their entire life. For them, it is more a matter of what is sensibly obvious than an article of faith. Hindus or Buddhists do not "believe" in transmigration in the sense the Christians believe, or are expected to believe, in the resurrection of the flesh. They seem to have a vivid, intense perception of it in spite of its obscurity. Many among them, for instance, will affirm that they can feel on their shoulders the "burden" of their accumulated previous lives. Moreover they are rarely seen to be searching for clues, omens or evidence.

Another typical feature of Indian transmigration is the essentially ethical character of the mechanism which it obeys. This is the principle of *karman*. This term, which originally indicated sacrifice or ritual action, ended up applying to any human behaviour one could qualify in terms of good or evil, or conformity or not with the *dharma*, i.e. the just order of things. Righteous action will earn its doer a "merit" (*puṇya*) which will bear fruit either in this life or in a future existence, in the form of various satisfactions; enjoyments, honours, wealth, etc. In the same way, unjust action results in a demerit (*pāpam*), which then brings multiple sufferings in this life or in another yet to come. And as there is an obvious link between the hierarchy of social conditions and that of satisfactions which individuals can expect from existence, the principle of *karman* will find expression in the first place through rebirths more or less noble or miserable, according to the overall ethical quality of deeds done during previous lives. This same tenet will also, in addition, determine multiple secondary factors contributing to happiness or unhappiness such as gender, physical constitution, robust or frail, and the seemingly fortunate or unfortunate encounters throughout one's life. And so what we have here is an absolute principle of immanent justice, although often delayed in its concrete actualization: sooner or later, everyone will get the experiences they deserve. An Indian saying states that an action will indeed find its way back to its doer even at the other end of the world, as surely as a cow will recognize its calf among a thousand others. We can take for granted that such a tenet, by stifling all attempts to fight "social injustice," has helped in a powerful way to strengthen the hereditary caste hierarchy. Moreover, by thus eliminating the scandal of "the Just who suffer," Indians have been spared having to grapple with the eternal problem of Evil, which has for so long — and nowadays more than ever — haunted European consciousness.

However, human rebirths on the various levels of the social order, from the untouchables to the brāhmaṇas, are not all that is at stake here. The distinctive feature of Indian *saṁsāra* is indeed its unfolding on a cosmic scale, on a huge "ladder of sentient beings," where humankind occupies only the middle rung. Above stand a host of superior beings: the countless gods, spirits and demi-gods constituting the pantheon of Hindu and Buddhist mythologies. Underneath come the animals, remote from humans in varying degrees, then plants and minerals. Although there are many subtle differences of opinion on this point, the predominant view is indeed that "souls" are not once and for all either divine, human, or animal, etc. but may assume any one of these conditions according to their *karman*. Thus it is possible, in the course of boundless time, to either rise to the rank of the gods, or to fall back into the misery and anonimity of the most insignificant of creatures. In all this, the human condition, however average or mediocre it be on the hierarchical scale, none the less remains a privileged one. All schools indeed agree in regarding this condition as the only one within which souls can act to shape their own future in one way or the other. "Above," the gods are too immersed in the delights of their heavenly existence to be likely to wish any alteration of their fate. And so they quietly and passively wait for their merits, which have earned them the exalted condition they are presently enjoying, to be exhausted. "Below," animal creatures are too sluggish, too paralysed by the relative coarseness of their organs, to be able to discriminate between what is just and what is unjust. And so they are restless, constantly tossed between desire and fear, but they do not act, strictly speaking, and thus do not generate any new good or bad *karman,* since this remains the privilege of humankind. Thus the tenet of *karman* appears poles apart from any fatalistic doctrine, inasmuch as it leads us to consider the statistically rare human condition as a precious opportunity given to souls to influence the course of their destiny. The transmigrating condition can thus be lived in a cheerful, affirmative, optimistic way, seen from the vantage point of this privileged human condition. The way indeed is all laid out: it will be enough in this world to abide by one's *dharma* in the most scrupulous way to retain, if not increase, in one's next existence, the advantages one already enjoys in this life. The untouchable himself, proclaims the *Bhagavad-Gītā*, will better his fate in his next life if he lawfully complies with the humble "duty of his stage of life" (*svadharma*).[3] And indeed it is hardly disputable that the moral life of the great majority of Indians nowadays still rests on the hopeful expectation of a better future rebirth, which is of course offset by the fear of a decline caused by certain demerits which one would not or could not have avoided in the present lifetime.

In spite of it all, the deeper meaning of the Indian ideas of *karman* and *saṁsāra* is to be sought in another direction — the one revealed by the presence, in the midst of traditional society, of individuals called "renunciants" (*saṁnyāsin*) among the Hindus, and "mendicant monks" (*bhikkhu*) among the Buddhists, figures whose immense prestige is linked to the very fact of their adopting a thoroughly negative attitude towards *saṁsāra*. The avowed goal of their asceticism is indeed not to be born ever again, to extricate oneself some day, once and for all, from this perpetual round of reincarnations, which they feel as bondage — in a word, to reach final liberation (*mokṣa, nirvāṇa*). This attitude which views any form of attachment to life, even in respecting one's *dharma*, as the expression of a blind desire and an ignorance of the true metaphysical calling of man, thus rendering on social life a globally "pessimistic" judgement, has left a lasting stamp on the whole of Indian civilization. For more than two millennia,

3. See for example III.35; IX.27-32; XVIII.45-49.

India has cultivated the image of transmigration as an aimless wandering, from birth to birth, in pursuit of the mirage of an inaccessible earthly happiness.[4]

Turning towards the Western reality of today, we shall ask whether it is possible, and if so, to what extent, to find there the characteristic features of Indian *karma* and *saṁsāra*. We will note first a certain similarity of language, sometimes even a true mimesis in terminology. Not only is the idea of *karman* itself regularly mentioned without always feeling the need of clarifying, but also certain more technical notions are being used in a causal way. For instance, Brāhmanic philosophy was very early on led to ponder the fact that the *ātman* (the "Self)" — itself outside space and time — could not, strictly speaking, transmigrate, that is to say, move through space and evolve through time. In search of the real transmigrating principle, it had been led to postulate the presence, inside the ordinary visible body, of a second body, also material but made of a certain subtle matter making it imperceptible as well as invulnerable to the operation of the gross physical agents (fire, water, etc.). It is to this subtle body (*sūkṣma śarīra* or *liṅga śarīra*) that the *ātman* would come to attach itself, under the sway of delusion, its connection to the ordinary gross body being effected only through this subtle body, and secondarily. It is there that the traces left by the course of experience — emotions, memories, habits, and acquired dispositions (*saṁskāra* and *vāsanā*) — would come to be imprinted. And it is this same subtle body which, surviving at

4. This point however would need to be qualified, inasmuch as recent ethnographical surveys conducted notably in south India, highlight here and there, among the "untouchables" or the very low castes, a certain mocking scepticism towards such a belief. The origin and social function of this attitude remain for the moment not well determined.

death the destruction of the gross body, would then implant itself in a newly formed embryo (following certain complex and abstruse procedures which have given rise to many a discussion between schools), thus assuring the transmigratory continuity of an individual existence, biological as well as psychological.

These same diverse notions are to be found again among Western transmigrationists today. The subtle body becomes for them, probably with the aid of spiritism, which, one century earlier, had taken over this vocabulary, the "astral body," or "fluidic body" or else "etheric." The only novelty here is probably the sporadic manifestation of a certain technological ambition quite characteristic of our times, which claims to detect in an objective way this subtle or etheric body with the help, by the way, of a whole jumble of scientific equipment (spectrometers, interferometers, Geiger counters, Kirlian photographic procedures, etc.). In the same way, the concepts of *vāsanā* and *saṁskāra* are today in common usage in these circles, probably due to the mass diffusion of Yoga in the West over the last thirty years and to a certain popularization of Freudian psychoanalysis which gives great importance to the notion of traces deposited "in the unconscious" by various traumatic childhood experiences.

But language is not everything, and the same notions can be invoked, the same formulas used, without the final message being identical for all that. And this, so it seems, is precisely what is occurring here. The first difference — which in fact implies all the others — is that transmigrationist beliefs, on the one hand, remain marginal in our civilization, in spite of their swiftly gaining ground, and on the other hand, are always the result of individual initiatives, even if these occur, here and there, within the framework of a sect or small group. In other words, in the modern West these beliefs are neither backed by strong collective support nor rooted in a powerful religious and philosophical tradition. Those who take them up are thus aware of being pioneers, breaking new ground at their own risk. But what is it that pushes them to go this way? Here there can be little doubt about the answer. If, in this early twenty-first century, belief in reincarnation seems to be in a position to conquer the West, it is because it appears to be carrying a message of hope. The vast literature devoted nowadays to the subject is, almost unintentionally, evidence of this. The prospect of a perhaps unlimited succession of future births, far from frightening our contemporaries, reassures them, for it presents itself to them above all as a promise of eternal life. Indeed for them, the choice is no longer between Heaven or Hell, salvation or damnation, but rather between pure and simple annihilation and reincarnation, however hypothetical and difficult to imagine it might be.

Thus contemporary neo-transmigrationist ideology appears indissociable from what it tends to replace: the old Christian eschatology of the Resurrection of the Flesh and Last Judgment. We shall return to this point later, but it is important right now to emphasize how remote these views are from traditional Indian conceptions. The Indians, or at least the most lucid among them, do not fear the obliteration of their ego at death, but, quite to the contrary, its indefinite perpetuation. To recall a famous metaphor, *saṁsāra* appears to them as "the Great Ocean, whose waves are the ever-recurring delusions and sufferings." Therefore they yearn to cross it once and for all in order to settle on "the other shore" of Liberation. And here we are poles apart from Western reincarnationism, which virtually ignores the very notion of Liberation and puts all its hopes into the indefinite prolongation of a series of rebirths yet to come.

Similar divergences show up as soon as one has to determine both the content and the meaning, as well as the possible end of the series of rebirths. The Indian view holds that the content encompasses all of the beings who populate the cosmos. All are supposed to be part of the vast movement of transmigration, and each one of them is supposed to be able to assume, in one phase or another of their destiny, any one of the possible conditions of reincarnation. This implies that there is no migratory stream flowing in one privileged direction, but only one vast disorderly fluctuation within which no irreversible transformation is ever looming, even in the long term. Sentient beings are tossed around indefinitely, now ascending, now descending the ladder of beings, according to their deeds. The gods themselves are very likely, once their merits are exhausted, to find themselves confined once more for millions of years in the miserable, repetitive existences of insects, worms, etc. The only irreversible movement conceivable within such a universe is precisely that which, taking human existence as a springboard, finds its outcome in Liberation. But if Liberation in one sense can be seen as the "natural locus" of the soul, the soul, nevertheless, was not promised Liberation from the beginning of time, or was not for ever destined to it. Therefore no sentient being is ever granted its salvation in advance. All risk seeing their imprisonment in the labyrinth of *saṁsāra* indefinitely prolonged, thus giving it a properly infernal character.

In contemporary Western presentations, on the contrary, it is almost always a matter of a directed future which is globally ascending. As a result, the possibility of animal rebirths will be either expressly denied or passed over in silence, or else in the best of cases relegated to an antediluvian past forever done with.[5] The more glamorous prospect of *post-mortem* ascensions towards mysterious supra-human conditions, on remote planets or in extra-galactic spaces worthy of science-fiction, is on the contrary easily envisioned.[6] The uppermost idea in all this is really that of life-lessons: one comes back to the world, on Earth or elsewhere, less to atone for past misdeeds than to work out unresolved psychical conflicts, or in order to better assimilate various moral or religious truths. At times there may be a real mission to be accomplished, by beings who have "reached a higher plane of evolution" and who come back among us in order to teach. Even the seeming lapses are no exception to this rule.

> The fashion designer Paco Rabane, for instance, believes he knows why he once reincarnated in the eighteenth century as a woman of easy virtue: "Having often (*sic*) been a priest, endowed with a certain power upon the minds of others, I was beginning to dry up. My heart had become callous, insensitive to my brothers' sufferings. In order to be uplifted, I had to know the fate of Marie-Magdeleine. I had to suffer the humiliation, the degradation, the public opprobrium.[7]

---

5. It is significant in this regard that already in antiquity, and particularly within Neoplatonism, the possibility of animal rebirths was hotly disputed and generally rejected. See H. Zander, op. cit., pp. 102-11.

6. The collective suicide committed in 1995 in Switzerland by members of the Knights of the Solar Temple sect fits right in here. H. Zander also mentions the case (p. 602) of the 38 members of the American religious community *Heaven's Gate,* who "took advantage" of the appearance of the Hale-Bopp Comet in 1997 to end their lives, apparently persuaded that the comet would take them into the infinity of the cosmos.

7. Paco Rabane, *Trajectoire,* Paris, 1991, p. 89.

In short, where traditional India imagines a truly hellish circle or cycle, the West is prone to imagine a sort of ascending spiral through which individual destinies would seem to be drawn and, passing through a thousand seeming catastrophes and tragedies, to be led ever nearer to the divine.

We have already said that Indian religious consciousness never felt the need to prove to itself the objective reality of transmigration (just as to this day for the great majority of us it seems unnecessary to build up proof for the immediate intuition we have of our present life as unique and non-repeatable). It is quite another matter for modern supporters of reincarnation, precisely because they have to struggle against a collective belief or unquestioned feeling which, quite the opposite, asserts that "one lives only once." That evidence, those signs or clues, which nineteenth-century spiritualists sought through levitating tables, our contemporaries believe they can find them in past-life memories, be they spontaneous or induced. In this regard there exist, in fact, two distinct approaches.

One of these wishes to be scientific and objective. It rests on the fact that in some regions of the globe and within certain milieus, some individuals, generally children or adolescents, suddenly "recognize" places which as a rule they are visiting for the first time, calling by name perfect strangers whom they pass in the street, listing the tastes, opinions and character traits of people deceased well before they themselves were born drawing a precise picture of long past events, generally tragic (old crimes, etc.), which they would not have been able to witness or hear about from anybody. It is then a matter of investigating on the spot, both as a sleuth and as a historian, scrutinizing the consistency of these stories, checking the alleged facts, the validity of the alleged evidence, etc. in order to eliminate all possibility of hoaxes or the presence of parallel sources of information which, in good faith, might not have been detected. In the small number of cases where the phenomenon does not yield to any of the many attempts at a "non-supernatural" explanation, the hypothesis of reincarnation can then, according to the advocates of this approach, be cautiously, tentatively advanced to account for them. Such is the method followed notably by the American Ian Stevenson and his followers. It does not assert the reality of reincarnation in a dogmatic way, but only its plausibility "in the present state of science."[8]

The second approach is internal. One might see in it the extrapolation of some methods of investigating the unconscious, all more or less directly derived from psychoanalysis (free association, directed dreaming, hypnotic suggestion, primal scream, etc.). The idea of using these methods to uncover possible previous lives was, it seems induced by two main factors. On the one hand, it was found possible to return in memory well beyond generally accepted limits (age 3-4), back to very early infancy and even to the intra-uterine state. On the other hand, the setting up of new reanimation techniques allowed many patients to be brought back to life who in the past would have been legitimately regarded as dead. Their testimony, whatever interpretation one may give to it, suggests that at both extreme ends of life, consciousness, far from being extinguished, on the contrary sees its powers exalted. Thus one could emphasize a certain continuity of the stream of consciousness from the very first moments of life (how many have thus relived, or thought they relived, the "trauma" of their birth!), to the moment of its

8. See Ian Stevenson, *Twenty Cases Suggestive of Reincarnation*, University of Virginia Press, 1974.

seeming extinction. The idea that consciousness would suddenly appear, in a miraculous way, at the very instant of birth in order to disappear, in no less sudden a fashion, at the instant of death, became thus less and less plausible. From then on, the way was open for tentative explorations of this stream of consciousness even beyond the limits of one's present existence, and the very ancient notion of "previous lives" came to give these still-budding researches a made-to-order frame of reference.

We shall not recall here the history of these researches, flourishing by the way as much in Europe as in the United States. Even today their achievements may seem fairly impressive. The methods of anamnesis are quite varied, and so are the practitioners: psychologists, psychoanalysts, clergy, physicians, *guru*s more or less famous, etc. Some use hypnosis, others deep relaxation, others suggestion within an adequate sensorial environment; a few do not hesitate to make use of hallucinogenic drugs like LSD. The purpose of these "trips" is most often therapeutic, at least at the beginning: searching the very remote pre-natal past for the origin of phobias, self-defeating patterns, and even organic troubles for which one finds no plausible explanation within the context of the present existence. But exploring the pre-empirical past can also become an end in itself. It is then, each time, a delving into the unknown: the subject can never know in advance in which of his countless previous lives he is going to "land." He soon finds himself confronted with visions and involved in scenes which he has first to locate in space and time before attempting to figure out their meaning. His "guide" tries to help him by asking questions such as: "Can you describe your body?" (male or female, young or old, etc.), "What kind of clothes do you wear?," "Which language is spoken by the people around you?," "Are they friendly or hostile towards you?," etc. Thus the evocation takes shape, and the subject really has the impression of reliving some episode, generally colourful and dramatic, of one of his previous lives. Tens of thousands of similar "trips" may thus already have been taken, most of them duly recorded on tape! And so we shall not be surprised to hear the supporters of these methods claiming publicly that reincarnation is today no longer a matter of belief but of direct experience.

If this were really the case, it is in fact, a complete shift of the religious consciousness, practically a metamorphosis of our civilization, that we would be facing. It is indeed all of our attitudes towards the future, towards work, love, politics, history which would be turned upside down if the reality of previous lives would become obvious or empirically verifiable by everyone. But we are not yet there, since a wide gap still separates the apparent content of these testimonies and the interpretation which some are eager to give. While going through these stories, indeed, one is struck to see that the previous lives thus brought back to the surface have nothing ordinary about them. That is, they are not very representative of what by necessity must have been the most common fate of humankind throughout the ages preceding our epoch. What do we know indeed of the large human groups who have populated the various continents during past centuries? How many were the tribes, ethnic groups, and peoples who left but very modest traces in history, and whose language, customs, rites, and beliefs are for ever buried in anonimity! Statistically, one should expect to see the re-emergence of countless destinies hard or impossible to identify, and belonging to this vast silent majority of humankind. Also, there should be plenty of lives of slaves, rural workers, maids, mercenaries, etc.

But the reality, if one can say so, is quite different. Simplifying somewhat, one can say that the destinies brought back to light by these diverse methods of anamnesis fall under two braod categories. First, what could be called emblematic functions or roles: high priests, high initiates, wonder-workers, vestal priestesses, Druids, Templars, inquisitors, ministers, high class courtesans, etc. A high proportion, perhaps the majority of the lives thus exhumed, have as their setting ancient Egypt — not surprisingly — but also Aztec Mexico, the Court of Frederic II in Palermo, the holy city of Benares, etc., all places endowed with religious or esoteric prestige.

The second category appears at first sight more heterogeneous, and so less liable to criticism. We find here a jumble of lives of peasants, aristocrats, merchants, soldiers, etc. most of which seem to have been lived in Europe or the Mediterranean Basin. Yet if one takes a close look at them, one realizes that they too are all but ordinary. These are lives, or rather violent deaths, of typical figures corresponding, if not to clichés or naïve representations, at least to vignettes from children's history books: Roman legionaries grappling with Barbarians or Carthaginians, gladiators, slaves rebelling under Spartacus, Christians thrown to the lions in the arena, witches burnt at the stake, Crusaders lost in the Syrian desert and hunted by Saracens, pirates of the Southern seas, aristocrats guillotined under the Revolution, Napoleon's soldiers trapped in the retreat from Russia, or else, closer to us, deportees to Nazi concentration camps.[9] On the other hand, vague, dull destinies, devoid of striking incidents, are lacking or under-

9. These examples, taken above all from the Francophone literature, naturally reflect a specific national imaginary, but the same features are found, *mutatis mutandis,* in Anglophone, Germanic, and other literature. See for example H. Zander, op. cit., pp. 624-28.

represented. Moreover, the subjects never seem to run into historic episodes with which they would not be acquainted in their conscious culture, whose particulars would be unknown to them, and which they would need to identify afterwards by looking into dictionaries and encyclopedias. The outside observer is thus led to suspect that these subjects, far from uncovering authentic previous lives, are only projecting various emotional contents of their unconscious on certain emblematic, if not archetypal, situations, which their historic culture puts at their disposal. Without wanting to prematurely judge the possible therapeutic interest of these practices, it is difficult to see in them an experimental confirmation of the principle of reincarnation.

II

One would at first glance be tempted to take more seriously Ian Stevenson's investigations, inasmuch as he conducts them with meticulous thoroughness and in a highly critical spirit, which led him precisely to accept only a few among the thousands of cases that he dealt with. Stevenson shows that he is clearly aware of the possibilities of "rational" explanation, for example on the grounds of indirect suggestion and cryptomnesia.[10] According to him, only those cases which consistently resist such explanations, would be likely to "suggest" the reality of reincarnation. Two orders of facts, however, contribute to weakening this hypothesis. On the one hand, nearly all of Stevenson's researches were conducted within cultural areas (India, Sri Lanka) or communities (the

10. Certain cases have been totally "demystified," like that of Bridey Murphy, which was widely talked about in the United States in the seventies. See Ian Wilson, *Mind out of Time? Reincarnation Claims Investigated*, V. Gollancz, London, 1981.

Druses of Lebanon) where transmigration is an unquestioned collective belief. There naturally results from this an unconscious and natural predisposition, on the part of the witnesses interviewed, to select their observations and to give their stories a slant which would agree with the general framework of reincarnation. One notes, on the other hand, that what is suspected to have been a given subject's most recent past life always takes place within a radius of about 15-20 km from his present residence. In the pure logic of moral retribution, of *karma*, this geographical limitation appears devoid of any justification. On the other hand it would agree fairly well with a sort of unconscious complicity, mutual osmosis among psyches, or at least partial interchangeability of gestures, spontaneous attitudes and reactions between people of the same religious group and especially of the same geographic region. It will be noticed, by the way, that Stevenson's "external" approach and the "internal" approach of the *guru*s of anamnesis contradict each other more than they complete or support each other, inasmuch as the first favours a certain "local" style of reincarnation, whereas the second leads most often to remote and exotic previous lives.

By these few critical remarks — which it would be of course possible to elaborate and systematize — we do not mean, however, to reduce this collection of phenomena of "journeys through time" to a vast collective illusion, still less to a deliberate mystification. More accurately, we do not deem it possible to interpret them only in terms of true and false. In a way, everything that concerns the beyond is indeed as a rule unverifiable, inasmuch as any observation or measurement made within that realm would *ipso facto* make it part of this world here below. We will thus propose that these stories of previous lives are neither true nor untrue, but that their proliferation in our epoch must meet a certain need of the collective psyche. Let us not forget that man's conscious life is incessantly surrounded by a cloud of psychic manifestations which remain an enigma for our understanding: dreams, hallucinations, auras, paramnesias, split personalities, impressions of *déja vu* etc. The extreme plasticity of these phenomena makes them liable to very diverse interpretations. Thus at certain times in cultural history, a need was felt to understand them in terms of messages emanating from the beyond. Religious literature of the Early Middle Ages, for example, is filled with apparitions and visionary stories: the damned souls from Purgatory, and also saints, appear suddenly to a monk, a lord, or a humble maid, urging them to lead a more Christian life, warning them against this or that individual, predicting the day and circumstances of their own death, sometimes taking them to visit a region of Heaven or Hell.[11] These kinds of stories have grown more scarce through the centuries, have become less and less credible, and have finally completely disappeared. Their decline is the very decline of a certain Christian imaginary, notably as to eschatology. And the vacuum which it has left behind is today being engulfed by another imaginary, by another way of translating into visions and stories the same material — timeless like the human psyche itself — of paranormal experiences and altered states of consciousness.

The present surge of transmigrationist ideas in the Western world calls for, it seems, a historic perspective. It yields itself to interpretation only over the longterm and from the perspective of the history of mentalities. What we witness today is indeed a resurgence, and not a radically new phenomenon. From the point of view of the historian and

---

11. Numerous examples in J. Le Goff, *La naissance du purgatoire*, Gallimard, Paris, 1983.

even more of the anthropologist, the eschatology of reincarnation has always been that of the majority on the planet, even if it has not assumed everywhere as "learned" and systematic a shape as in ancient India and in the countries of Buddhist civilization — and it is much more the resurrectionist eschatology, peculiar to the three "religions of the Book:" Judaism, Christianity, Islam, which represents the exception and the enigma. In Europe itself, transmigration is nothing new. Its extremely rich and complex history is today just beginning to be investigated in a systematic way. But in fact, a red thread, subtle but uninterrupted, connects Pythagoras and Empedocles[12] to Victor Hugo through Origenism, the Cathars, the Kabbala, Giordano Bruno, Lessing, Goethe, German Romanticism, etc. For a long time marginal, almost clandestine because reputed to be heretical, transmigration appears in broad daylight only around the end of the eighteenth century, with the gradual ossification of traditional Christian eschatology. From then on, and throughout the nineteenth century, a whole lineage of thinkers and writers would defend it from the perspective of a progressive and optimistic philosophy of history, their guiding principle being that the host of humans who died "too early," during the centuries of ignorance and barbarism, must be given the chance to be reborn from age to age in order to have their share of the human progress achieved after them.[13] The contemporary curiosity for previous lives represents still

12. One recalls Fragment 117: "For in the past I was a young man and a young maiden and a shrub and a bird and a mute fish of the sea" (H. Diels/W. Kranz, *Die Fragmente der Vorsokratiker*, Zwölfte Auflage, Zürich-Dublin, 1966, vol. I, p. 358).

13. See H.de Lubac, *La postérité spirituelle de Joachim de Flore*, Le Sycomore, Namur-Paris, 2 vol. 1978 et 1981; also G. Gusdorf, *Du Néant ā Dieu dans le savoir romantique*, Payot, Paris, 1983.

another version of this same belief, whose inflated individualism and narcissism can easily be explained by the collapse of progressivist dreams and the magnitude of the historic catastrophes of the twentieth century.

One could consider that the obviously fanciful, if not outright delirious, aspects which in many cases the new belief in transmigration reveals, are above all a sign of the mental disarray of those who adopt it, which would disqualify it in advance as a vision of the world which has a future. None the less the history of religions gives us many examples of great spiritual movements which began in a confused turmoil of this kind, yet eventually led to enduring transformations of collective myths and practices. In fact, it would seem that spontaneous and unorganized change in attitudinal patterns almost always paves the way for the big shifts of conceptual thought. Most often, the impulse comes from below, and finds itself afterwards captured and mulded by philosophical or theological reflection. Now in the present time, several objective factors seem to favour, over the middle and long-term, a return to the foreground of the idea of transmigration. These factors are of a theorical, ethico-religious, and social order.

Indeed a certain image of the world, inherited in part from antiquity, in part from the Middle Ages, constituted for a long time a natural framework for the eschatology of the Resurrection and Last Judgement. It set man apart, infinitely above the other living beings, and his habitat, the earth, at the centre of the universe. It rested on a short time span of about a few thousand years between the creation and the end of the world. This image of the world is now outdated. Geocentrism was the first to collapse. Anthropocentrism followed, undermined on the one hand by the emphasis put, beginning with Darwin, on a real process of becoming human spread over at least three million years, and on the other hand, by ethology, which revealed the full extent of the behavioural kinship between man and certain higher animals. Finally, contemporary cosmology has moved back the coming to birth of the universe by 15 or 20 billion years, has left open the prospect of an unlimited future expansion of the universe, and in any case envisions a possible "end of the world" only billions of years from now, and this in such physical conditions that the event will no longer have any conceivable link with the waning of human history on the planet earth. The ancient doctrines of Hinduism and Mahāyāna Buddhism — which were prone to see creatures transmigrating from world to world and embracing in succession all possible conditions against a background of boundless cosmic and at the same time "imaginary" space and time — thus happen to be once again relevant, and to resonate as they never did in the past of Western culture.

But in addition to this theoretical interest there is also another, ethico-religious. The conception, or rather *perception*, of human life as unique and non-repeatable led inevitably to a "Manichean" eschatology of salvation and damnation, both final. The precise content of these last two representations could, within Christianity itself, vary in the course of the centuries; but their structural opposition was to maintain itself, in spite of its seeming alleviation by Limbo or Purgatory. Now, our contemporaries can hardly any longer support a religious anthropology which, without necessarily making a simplistic division of humankind into "good" and "evil," none the less admitted that ultimately or "in God's Judgement," some would see their misdeeds forgiven, but not others. Today, psychoanalysis and depth psychology in general have made us more sensitive to the infinite complexity of the human psyche, to the extreme ambiguity of the motivations behind any behaviour, and to the determining role of chance events in shaping one's personality and crystallizing one's major life options. We are now prone to think that the meaning of a life is not exhausted by the materiality of its observable behaviours, that it is constantly evolving and is as if left hanging, up to the very instant when death arrives to arbitrarily freeze it as destiny. In short, we no longer really believe in the possibility, "even for God," of passing a final and irrevocable judgement, one way or the other, on a life which has just ended. In a way, the "verdict" of transmigration, pronounced automatically, in the absence of any Supreme Judge, can appear more equitable to the extent that it supposedly takes into account one's merits as well as demerits, distributes only relative, time-limited, punishments and rewards, and thus leaves open this field of possibilities, that of any human destiny, essentially unfinished at death.

A third motivating factor — this time, of a social or socio-ethical order — tends to induce a return to favour of the idea of reincarnation. The inequality of opportunities at birth, which has of course always and everywhere existed, is nowadays perceived more acutely than ever, and this at the very moment when throughout the world political powers, at least those among them that are not totalitarian, acknowledge they have at their disposal only palliative remedies in order to fight this evil. Here also, biology and the social sciences have played a role by highlighting the fact that it is very early, indeed in the very first years of life, that chances for success in life, in the conventional sense, can be jeopardized or else on the contrary, enhanced. It is known today that the young child's diet conditions the maturation of his or her brain. A diet deficient in certain trace elements during the first three or four years will result for the adult in an irremediable intellectual deficit. A lack of sensory stimulation or affection will have a still more devastating impact. Now these different factors in turn obviously depend on the country of birth, historic conditions (peace or wartime), the parents' social milieu, the relative harmony or discord in their relationship, etc. On another level, the sociology of education emphasizes that children entering school do not rank equally; besides possible hereditary biological factors, the cultural environment in the home plays an important, some say decisive, background role with regard to their future academic success or failure.

Now these diverse sources of inequality are beginning to be seen in a more and more stark light, since all the hopes which the masses throughout the world had invested in a mythical Revolution supposedly capable of attacking the root of this evil and eventually suppressing it once and for all, have little by little been fading over the last decades. On the contrary it is nowadays a commonly accepted idea that a certain degree of inequality is necessary for the smooth functioning of society, in any case of the economy, since any strictly egalitarian policy would result in a race to the bottom, with demoralizing effects for the best and most enterprising individuals. Faced with this problem, without really daring to acknowledge it, governments now limit their ambitions to correcting somehow the most glaring inequalities.

However, for any eschatology resting on the principle that "one lives only once," the fact of being born in a given place on the planet, in a given family and social milieu, is an element without particular significance, indeed utterly fortuitous. The enormous inequality of opportunities at birth, which it seems beyond human means to remedy, necessarily then appears an enigma and an outrage. Hence the temptation for a conscience tormented by this state of things — and their number is most likely to multiply in the future — to fall back on the old idea of transmigration, which makes of the mystery of evil a problem, for which it proposes a vaguely rational answer.

Thus transmigration, after having preceded Christianity and having under its rule remained as a parallel eschatology, in its shadow, may find itself today in the position of surviving it. Its perennial character is probably due to the simple, intuitive ways in which it imitates the cycles of nature: seasonal rhythms, migrations of birds, metamorphosis of insects, the regular alternation of generation and corruption. "The belief in metempsychosis" writes Schopenhauer "appears as man's natural conviction, as soon as, without preconceived idea, he begins somewhat to reflect."[14] Indeed, we may be heading towards a new paradigm, or towards the renovation of a very old one, while a long historical parenthesis may be in the process of closing. Two or three centuries from now, perhaps, the idea of an infinite succession of rebirths will again have imposed itself as compellingly self-evident.

Does this mean that reincarnation will then have the status of a proven and thenceforth indisputable scientific truth? In no way. To imagine this would mean to apply the logical principle of the "excluded middle" to a realm which by its very nature lies outside its rule. It is "obvious" to our understanding that existence is either unique or multiple, without a conceivable middle ground. Thus, either the hypothesis of transmigration will be true and that of the single non-repeatable existence false, or the opposite. Now if this same understanding, taking into account a possible limitation

---

14. *Le monde comme volonté et représentation*, PUF, Paris, 1966, p. 1255; also see pp. 447-49.

of our ability to know in these matters, affirms that one hypothesis is only probable, and the other proportionately improbable, or even if it concludes that the question is indecidable and rejects equally both hypotheses, it none the less continues tacitly to postulate that "in Reality itself," in the "Thing in itself," as unrecognizable as that is for us, it is "necessarily" one or the other hypothesis which finds itself verified. But to reason like this is to forget that the screen of death is by definition opaque. And such an opacity is absolute, for if we could really, by appropriate means, cast a glance at the afterlife and in some way communicate with the dead, this would imply a real integration of the space-time beyond with our space-time here below, and thus a real dissolution of death. Let us return for a moment to ancient India. It has always been known there that the idea of *saṁsāra* corresponds only to an exoteric or "popular" level of truth, and that behind it, another more esoteric truth was to be sought. This is the very meaning of the idea of Liberation as it is presented, for example, in Non-Dualistic Vedānta and Mahāyāna Buddhism. In Vedānta it is more particularly the paradigm of the dream which predominates: access to Liberation takes place in the course of the adept's "last" incarnation, just as in a dream, especially a nightmare, waking up is induced by an ultimate dream episode of unbearably dramatic character. And just as in retrospect awakening disqualifies as pure illusions all of the dream episodes which came before, in the same way Liberation subverts the very logic of transmigration and expresses itself by an insight such as this: "No one has ever been, is or will be in bondage to *saṁsāra*; all have been liberated from all eternity."[15] The only reality acknowledged for

---

15. Concerning the relevance of this same theme in Buddhism and Jainism, see W. Halbfass, *Karma and Wiedergeburt im indischen Denken*, Diederichs Kreuzlingen-München, 2000, pp. 70, 128, 225.

transmigration is, when all is said and done, a psychological or ethical one. It is not a wandering from body to body throughout the external world, but rather the internal odyssey of the soul, in the grip of the illusion that it is different from others, and which unconsciously strives by projecting itself into all kinds of imaginary situations and roles, to get rid of its congenital ignorance in order to join the universal Self. What is there "after" Liberation? A history has unfolded, but it is not that of a character who would survive the completion of his story and could sum it up to himself. Still the texts — Brāhmanic and Buddhist — evoke such a recapitulation, in the form of a "panoramic" reminiscence of previous lives supposedly taking place just before Awakening, but they understand it as the ultimate expression, half real, half unreal, the swan song of an apparent individual existence which is now returning to this immutable and pacified ground from which it appeared to have detached itself. One measures the abyss which separates these Indian conceptions from the contemporary neo-reincarnationism. On one side, a sort of flash which both illumines and consumes all of the previous pseudo-existences, a bridge thrown between time and eternity; on the other, a sort of fishing in the murky waters of the past which brings back haphazardly some previous lives, each more glamorous and glittering than the last.

Transmigration on the one hand, and the conception of life as unique and non-repeatable on the other, are thus in no way theories concerning the Real, nor do they attempt to approach it through reasoning and experience, which would make them demonstrable or refutable by means of those very sources of knowledge. They are collective mental constructions which precede and frame our conception of time and therefore dismiss in advance any fact of experience likely to contradict them. Their "truth" is not measured by their degree of adequacy to a hypothetical hidden Reality of how things might be after death, but by their capacity for opening to individuals positive and meaningful prospects, both for their present earthly existence and for the future which they cannot help imagining, beyond it.[16] They are "true" only inasmuch as they do perform this function, and they become "false," or rather inadequate, when they don't. Thus transmigration will play all the better its role of consoling belief to the extent that its mode of operation will be maintained in a darkness suitable to all individual emotional projections. On the contrary, when elevated in broad daylight as a dogma, a system for explaining and justifying everything, it immediately provokes a kind of outrage, both intellectual and moral. This could be seen quite recently in Germany, when certain reincarnationist "therapists"[17] did not hesitate to assert that the victims of the Nazi concentration camps, more particularly the Jews, had simply settled in the gas chambers, each one for themselves, a heavy murderer's *karma*.

---

16. From a more particularly philosophic perspective, it is possible to maintain that the structure of human temporality is such that a double reference to a past and a future is a component of any experienced present. In the grip of this transcendental imagination the man or woman, having reached the threshold of death, necessarily continues, even if he or she claims to be an atheist, to project a future, even if he or she calls it "Nothingness." Only the subversion of this radical imagination, i.e. the irruption of the eternal present of *nirvāṇa,* would be able to dissipate the mirage of the beyond as "future life."

17. Some of them were condemned in Frankfurt in 1996, at the close of a proceeding for libel filed by the Jewish community of Hesse. In the same way, the well-known American psychic Edgar Cayce maintained that "the sufferings inflicted on the Jews by the Nazis were but the kārmic consequence of the cruelty which the Jewish people had shown towards other communities in the course of history" (according to H. Zander, op. cit., p. 198 et p. 583.)

Let us conclude that, in any case, transmigration will perhaps be able in the future to compel recognition only inasmuch as it will be able to become, or become once more, the natural horizon of our consciousness of time. As a pure intellectual construction, it is flimsy, even dangerous. Its only possible reality is that of a massive collective certitude, in short, of a myth. Searching for objective proofs of it is pointless, and so is the ambition of refuting it with the help of rational arguments.

6

Morals and Soteriology

Michel Hulin

Introduction

IN classical India the notion of *karman* cannot be separated from that of *saṁsāra* which means metempsychosis or indefinite transmigration of beings from rebirth to rebirth. More precisely *karman* is what, in a Hindu or Buddhist context, gives its specific meaning to the widely, if not universally, held belief in some form of reincarnation. For the notion includes an idea of compensation for actions committed in previous lives — good rebirths rewarding moral actions, bad rebirths punishing immoral ones — an idea which is not to be found anywhere else. True, many primitive societies know of different ways for the dead to "come back" among the living but, with them, this characteristic ethical connotation is not to be found. In most cases, it is rather a means used by an ideology aiming at strengthening the cohesion of the group through a link with its ancestors. In the modern West the ideas of *karman* and *saṁsāra* have certainly gradually become familiar but they are seen from a point of view unknown in ancient India, that of a continuous spiritual progress. This study plans to deal with the structure and function of the notion but will not broach the question of its century-long dark genesis. In the same way it will be centred on the rather classical version of the doctrine, such as it is being taken for granted (rather than proven) in the major texts of Hinduism, Buddhism and Jainism. One more remark : though this belief has been massively dominating the whole subcontinent for over two millennia, it has never been unanimously accepted. In the so-called lower castes it has always been received with a certain amount of scepticism and was even sometimes openly rejected. As a consequence, it should be considered as a vision of the world typical of the upper castes, those who can express themselves in Sanskrit and, first among them, of the brāhmaṇas.

The Presuppositions of the Doctrine

The classical doctrine of *karman*, developed in reference books, is based upon a small number of axioms which are seldom stated as such, because they make up the presuppositions shared by all those who take part in such discussions. In a rather simplified way one can perceive five of them :

1. The eternal and uncreated character — the one implying the other — of the conscious principle present within any living being, human or other. Despite appearances, such a form of extant existence profoundly differs from the Christian immortality of the soul which implies its creation by God and its possible annihilation by Him. Such a rule will apply not only to the Self of the Upaniṣads and classical Brāhmanic philosophies but also to the series of moments of consciousness, its equivalent in a Buddhist context. With regard to a given individual existence, that is to an incarnation, this entity is supposed to underly it and, also, to pre-exist and survive to it.

2. In the same way and from all eternity this principle would be ignorant of its proper nature. And this original ignorance appears as a failure to recognize its essential attributes : infinity in time and space, omniscience, omnipotence, bliss, etc. In a concrete way this infinitude is brought down to the dimensions of the very body and of its limited powers — sensibility, locomotion, etc. The transcendent Self is thus metamorphosed — or rather appears, from all eternity, transformed — into an individual concrete ego inserted in a definite physical, psychological and social situation. As a consequence, it is confronted by the primitive prototypal form of good and evil, in the guise of pleasure and pain, that is what the body feels as favourable or unfavourable to its physiological well-being, its functional integrity and, lastly, its survival.

3. Because of this very ignorance which defines and separates them, beings appear primarily moved by the desire to assert themselves, each in its own particular way. For they are caught in a contradiction: on the one hand they are aware of their limited individuality, on the other they retain some sort of dark consciousness of their divine essence; hence a fundamental self-centredness which cannot be reduced to any form of determination linked to individual psychology or temper. Everyone tries, for his part, to obtain the maximal pleasure and suffer the minimal pain. To this purpose, beings are doomed to live in a latent or declared state of war; hence the pessimistic postulate of the pre-eminence of suffering in existence.

4. There exists in the universe some sort of moral order besides its properly physical order — the Sanskrit

word *dharma* meaning both things together. In the specifically moral order of things, *dharma* includes the notion of a just hierarchy — and especially between castes — as well as that of everyone carrying out his own duty, whatever his personal wishes may be — the duty pertaining to his position being his personal contribution to the general well-being through actions in keeping with his sex, his knowledge, his social position, etc. In return *dharma* demands that everybody should be rewarded for his dedication to the general welfare and punished for his lack of it. Now, in this our world, we daily watch the suffering of honest people and the insolent triumph of evil-doers. Thus there cannot but exist another dimension to existence in which this apparent scandal finds an explanation. This is where the fundamental principle of *karman* plays its part. According to this principle, every action will be rewarded in terms of happiness or unhappiness according to its being in conformity or not with the *dharma*. In a similar way, Kant defined the Sovereign Good as the perfect adequation of virtue and happiness and introduced the "Postulates of Practical Reason" — that is God, Freedom of the will and Immortality of the soul — as conditions which make this adequation possible in the future. From the Indian point of view, this principle can be equated to the idea according to which every present happiness, even that of evil-doers, and every present unhappiness, even that of good men, is due to actions, performed in the past, either in conformity with the *dharma*, or otherwise.

5. In so much as human actions most generally need to find their reward beyond the limits of our present existence, the notion of *karman* naturally leads to that

of *saṁsāra*. In the same way, however, beings are concerned by the *dharma* — in its proper ethical meaning, and its punitive dimension — merely to the extent in which they harbour ambitions and desires that are themselves possible only on the basis of original ignorance. Even a behaviour most respectful of *dharma* supposes this ignorance to the extent in which the subject, although complying with moral law, experiences it as a restraint to his spontaneous attractions and repulsions. That's why virtue can by itself only lead to extend indefinitely the number of good rebirths without definitely overcoming the suffering inherent to existence as such. For that reason the question will sooner or later be asked of the possibility of overcoming original ignorance, to what conditions and with what existential consequences. In other words, the problematics of *saṁsāra* lead to those of its possible ending. That notion of a final end to transmigration, along with the release it might procure, is, in Buddhist contexts, expressed by the term of *nirvāṇa* and, in Brāhmanic contexts, by those of those of *mokṣa* and *mukti*.

Karman as a Cosmic Mechanism of Retribution

Fundamentally, *karman* functions as a principle of immanent though differed retribution. "Immanent," means there is no "Judge of the dead," no "Tribunal of the next world" — (although some popular representations go in that direction but without questioning the principle of automatic retribution). "Differed," because the positive or negative sanction may take place within the existence during which the said action was carried out or, just as well, in the immediately following existence or any other still to come in the future. Hence, according to their acquired worth and unworth, souls will be reincarnated on the different degrees of the continuous scale of beings. Rebirths are therefore thought to be possible at all levels of the hierarchy of living beings, from the meanest animals — sometimes even the plants — to all sorts of beings superior to man, the gods included. The human race, standing in a middle position on this scale, is itself subdivided into various "births," corresponding to the hierarchy of castes. However, none of these conditions is final, for worth and unworth are limited, so that even the gods may, in the end, fall from a divine condition which was not theirs by nature but had been acquired through exceptionally deserving actions. In the same way, beings fallen into any low condition can always rise again on the hierarchical scale in the course of future rebirths. Yet this is a rather complex and controversial question. According to some, such beings will, anyway, have to be reborn in the human condition in order to acquire special merits, while, according to others, they are able to do so even in their infrahuman condition.

This principle being once stated, to apply it to experience is extremely difficult. For the basic problem lies in the difficulty to reconcile two apparently incommensurable types of causality. More precisely, to account for a happy or unhappy given event, for instance an accident, you must explain how a past bad action can mature or bear fruit through a whole play of psychic, social, and also mechanical, meteorological factors. and so on. How can we understand that an action committed in some distant previous life — maybe a mere bad intention — can pick out such a wide range of factors and make them converge on this very place, at this very time ? And, indeed, the difficulty is the same whether you adhere to an "atomistic" conception of kārmic retribution — according to which this or that single action leads to this or that particular pleasant or unpleasant retribution — or to a holistic conception — according to which it's the final balance of a life, in terms of positive and negative factors, that will globally determine the next reincarnation. And still we do not take into account the fact that any concrete human situation implies the intersection of many individual series, each of them being guided in its development by the ongoing maturation of its own *karman*. No wonder then that, facing the practical impossibility to unravel such skeins, Indian thought has, sometimes, specially in the realms of astrology and medicine, shown a propensity to set up the *karman* of an individual as an independent factor, next to the others — physical, social, etc. — which, together with it, determine his fate. Such a vast cosmic mechanism of retribution — which, in principle, was destined to get rid of all possibility of good or bad chance in human existence — becomes, then, a real *deus ex machina* perpetually invoked whenever the individual is confronted with happy or lamentable events whose actual "physico-ethical" genesis cannot be traced.

Karman as Self-creation

Facing such enigmas, the religious thinkers of ancient India have gradually followed another course. Giving up the project of disassembling the intricate machinery of *karman* — the complexity of which baffles anyway human understanding — they turned away from such an intellectual, objectivistic construction and chose to try and understand from within — that is in a psychological and existential way — how our actions could and should, sooner or later, fall back on us. The most important concept formulated within this prospect was that of the "subtle body," a material structure present within the organism and of a texture so delicate that it escapes the senses — hence its name "subtle" — as well as the destructive action of external agents — fire, water, etc. As the origin of the cerebral mechanisms of sensation, memory, voluntary motion, such a structure is supposed to store traces or impressions — called *saṁskāra* or *vāsanā* — of all that we experience from the physical and social world: affects, emotional reactions, desires, projects, etc. Registering thus the experience accumulated throughout a life, the subtle body survives the decay or the cremation of the so-called "gross" body *sthūla*. And, bearing all the engrams laid by the immediately preceding life this subtle body will plant itself into a newly formed embryo. Much thought has been devoted to understand the way in which this transplant takes place. We cannot enter into the details of these speculations. The main thing is to know that the subtle body is supposed to "choose" an embryo belonging to a species — *jāti* or condition of birth — whose mode of life is in keeping with the affinities — tastes, curiosities, aversions, etc. — developed during its previous lives, and specially during the last one. To this subtle body, wrapped in a nurtured gross body, is owed the ontological and psychological continuity between two successive incarnations — the twofold traumatism of death and birth being called for to account for the usual absence of explicit memories from the preceding existence. In a similar way, the presence in a very young child of innate dispositions and tendencies will be interpreted as the first manifestation of impressions left by previous lives on his subtle body.

And thus, through this notion of the subtle body, the Indian thought becomes gradually aware of the radically immanent quality of kārmic retribution. We then begin to understand that original ignorance cannot be likened to some sort of fate linking the individual to the *saṁsāra*, but that it rules over him with his very complicity. This idea can already be found in the texts of ancient Buddhism. Showing the concatenation of factors leading from one existence to the other, they put forward the infernal couple Desire — litt. Thirst and Ignorance, which is to be taken in a nearly mechanical meaning (sense): we are the prey of desires to the extent in which we are ignorant of our true nature, and, conversely, the urge of desires deters us from any effort to overcome our ignorance. This is the couple which, applied to it, moves the "wheel" of the *saṁsāra*. On the whole, what happens to each one of us is not so much in accordance with his deserts — to the judgement of some transcendent Power — as with his likings."what happens to each one of us is not so much in accordance with his deserts — to the judgement of some transcendent Power — as with his likings. Our joys and our sorrows, our successes and our failures, do not come from heaven, sent by the gods, as rewards or punishments; they were slowly, unconsciously prepared by the evolution of our psyche, day by day "choosing" the sort of relation to the world in which, rightly or wrongly, we felt better. And this would be tantamount to the Greek saying: "character is fate."

And thus we can see how inadequate are the "fatalistic" views of *karman*, nowadays still so frequent in the West — and even in India. They would be justified if, besides the emotional experiences presently lived through — which can actually be interpreted in terms of pure kārmic retribution — our very decisions made in the present were imposed to us by our heavy kārmic inheritance, that is by the motion of tendencies formed in previous lives. In such a case the notions of worthy and unworthy — the very basis of the idea of *karma* — would be deprived of all meaning. Indians are quite aware of that. For, indeed, they regularly oppose *daiva* — litt.

Whatever is ordained by the gods, that is chance, fate — and *puruṣakāra*, human action, the free human reaction to external events. This leads us to consider the human condition as shielded from determinism and hence privileged when compared to the animal condition and to the divine condition. For these two are considered as mere "places of kārmic retribution" (*bhogabhūmi*), whereas the human condition is also a "place of action" (*karmabhūmi*), that is a rare and precious way of living in which beings can act in the full sense of the term and, so, inflect the course of their fate one way or the other.

The Prospect of Release

In traditional India freedom does not only mean free will here and now, that is the formal power to choose one type of behaviour rather than another. It also, and more strongly, means the capacity to overcome original ignorance, the capacity to prevent it from pulling the strings, the ability to fight against it, ideally to win. In Buddhism, for instance, it appears as the ability to replace the cursed couple Desire/Ignorance by the virtuous one Detachment/Wisdom. Which means that against formal freedom stands out real concrete freedom, the ability once and for all to tear oneself away from a hazardous existence, in other words to achieve release. However, the other side of this awareness is the ability, also recognized by Indian thinkers, to deliberately remain immersed in original ignorance, even though considering this attitude just as a temporarily comfortable one.

Indeed, we already saw that, according to the doctrine of *karma*, merely "virtuous" actions, those that are in conformity with the *dharma*, are also, though in a minor degree, born from fundamental ignorance — hence a typically Indian existential dilemma between a so-called virtuous life, conforming to socially recognized ethical values, and the heroic radical indifference to all wordly or social values. In the first case, the individual should live a blameless life and fulfil all the duties pertaining to his position the aim being to obtain a following rebirth on a level equal to, or even higher than the present one, a sort of deferred social promotion. From this point of view, release remains some distant, abstract goal and may be more frightening than really wished for. From the other point of view, release, at the contrary, becomes some sort of obsession, of fixed idea to which one is ready to sacrifice all one's earthly possessions. That is the traditional way of renunciation — *saṁnyāsa* — through which one breaks away from society, seen as a place of desires and ambitions. As can easily be imagined, the first way has, in all times, been preferred by most Indians. Its followers do not formally repudiate the ideal of release but do not profess it "genuinely" — hence a special turn of mind which Westerners, both despising and envying it, have often described as an odd mixture of complacent optimism, conformism, fatalism and smiling indolence. There and then is *karman* most often called forth as the readymade explanation for individual and collective disasters and as a convenient reason not to act in order to prevent or amend them.

As to the second attitude, that which directly works for release through voluntarily relinquishing one's property, practising askesis, silence, meditation, it gave birth to a whole body of dialectics which may be considered as the foremost advanced Indian thought about soteriology. Indeed, the accumlated experience of centuries of spiritual practice enabled some thinkers to understand that the very fact of aiming at release and, therefrom, expect the "final ending of suffering" or "eternal bliss," was still a product of the pair thirst/ignorance, was but a new and higher form of self-preservation and self-assertion. On the other hand, however, merely to lose heart and abandon the search for release leads obviously nowhere hence the "dialectical" solution which, gradually, forced itself with Buddhists and brāhmins. To start with aiming at release as a goal, though knowing that this is still an impure desire and, on the way, to gradually transform the quest into an awareness of one's present and past freedom, to become aware that one has always been free and released. Paradoxically, release takes place, once or again, only when all the efforts to reach it have proved in vain. From that point of view, it is less the empirical ending of *saṁsāra* — which cannot anyway be verified — than the dispelling, in the released mind, of the mirage it consisted in.

Conclusion

When the pair *saṁsāra-nirvāṇa* loses all reality, *karman* does the same. It is therefore advisable to stay aloof from its so-called position as a scientific theory, that could be verified, or falsified by means of empirical observations. The vast socio-cosmic panorama depicting the worldwide motion of beings from rebirth to rebirth, according to their good and bad actions is but an illusion. In reality, everything takes place in the mind of him that, in his search for release, first needs this theoretical scaffolding, even if he will let it fall once his quest is over. *Karman* looks more like a Kantian "regulating idea" or, more simply, like a great myth that has the capacity of throwing some light on the human condition. For it mainly teaches us that every good or bad thing happening to us was, in reality, the result of our past intentions, even though we are, to say the least, not able to recall the inner steps that have led us to them. Contemplated from the point of view of the past, *karman* seems to be made of our old decisions, reified since a long time, having become part of the world, and gifted with a *vis inertiae* that makes them bounce back upon us like a boomerang. The notion will still ring true whether the so-called previous lives are real or not. As for the present and the future, the notion of *karman* boils down to an invitation to rely only on oneself to change one's destiny towards release or salvation and, specially, to no longer take shelter behind "unjust fate" or "bad luck," like being born unhealthy, or crippled, or in an unfavourable familial, social, historical setting, etc. According to this interiorized conception, to believe in *karman* simply means doing away with every "If it were not for"; and assuming our present condition, however unfortunate it may, at first sight, appear.

7

Karman in Medical Literature

Michel Hulin

Introduction

WITH Āyurveda we face a much less abstract, theoretical or "ideological" aspect of the *karman*. Its purpose is less to account, in moral and religious terms, for the unequal distribution of fortune and misfortune among men than, in order to explain the apparent injustices, to adapt this great principle to the needs of daily human action. Indeed, if we consider that our kārmic balance constitutes the ultimate cause of the fortune and misfortune we meet with in this life, such a rule cannot but apply to health, the ultimate good, and to illness and bodily disabilities of all sorts, the ultimate evil. But, on the other hand, if the kārmic determination of health and of its failures was to be understood in a fatalistic way, what part would medicine — that is the diagnosis, prevention and treatment of diseases — then play ? The *karman* of a given individual would infallibly be, in his body, the cause of such a disease, however carefully he would try to avoid it. Whereas the *karman* of another would certainly enable him to escape the disease, however careless he might be. In the same way, the evolution of the disease — its partial or total, quick or slow, cure or, even, its fatal conclusion — would not depend on the doctor and his therapeutical efforts. To this end, the founding fathers of Indian medicine — Caraka, Suśruta and a few others, in the very first centuries of this era — had to find a way to compromise with this religious rule whose validity they never thought to contest. Their reservations were above all about the deterministic/fatalistic interpretation of *karman* as, for instance, it clearly comes out from the following text :

> If the lifespan of all individuals is predetermined, then, with a view to the maintenance of health, one need not resort to drugs, medical herbs, vows, atonement, fasting, etc. One should not beware of fierce and excited beasts, elephants, camels or bulls. One should not be afraid of chasms or impassable stretches of water. One should not be afraid of fire, poisons, madmen, or of the king's rage. If the lifespan is predetermined one should not be afraid of premature death. Conversely, one should not try to obtain longevity, as that would be useless. But, in fact, experience always teaches us that those who go in for a battle are more likely to be killed than those who do not fight. In the same way, wholesome regimens in keeping with the climate and the seasons, proper food preparations, avoidance of excesses, lead those who keep these rules to longevity. — Caraka, III.3.36

Fate and Human Initiative

Such considerations very early led Indian thinkers to work out a pair of notions not only to be found in medical literature but also in other texts, and first among them, in the great epic *Mahābhārata*. It consists in the opposition *daiva/puruṣa-kara*. *Daiva* literally means what comes to us from above — from the gods — and corresponds to what we usually call fate, that is a transcendent opaque Power which bestows us a happy or unhappy destiny, sometimes the one, sometimes the other, without enabling us to understand the cause for its action. In front of these "decrees of fate," *puruṣa-kara*, literally "human action," stands for human initiative, the human answer to the blows of fate. If, indeed, in an Indian context, *daiva* is nothing but another word for *karman* with its fatalistic meaning, we must not forget that the term *puruṣa-kara* comes from the same root as *karman*. That is why, seen in the light of Āyurveda, these two terms cease to be absolutely opposed but belong to the field of "psycho-sociology" rather than to that of ethics or religion. *Puruṣa-kara*, of course, means the combined efforts of the doctor and his patient to restore impaired health; these could not possibly be efficient if diets, massages, medicines, surgery, etc. had to fight a kārmic causality which, belonging to another dimension, would be, by essence, out of the reach of any material or technical action.

Things are entirely different from the moment when *karman*, as a whole group of already achieved, already actual, social, psychical, physiological conditions, is itself understood from the point of view of *puruṣa-kara*. From a medical point of view, indeed, it is usually believed that, properly speaking, there is no "unexpected disease" but that diseases and disabilities are — always ? — the result of lack of hygiene, carelessness and wrong diet. To this extent, doctors, in their way, share in this great tendency to interiorize *karman*, mentioned in another lecture, which tendency consists in deciding that what appears, to our eyes, as incomprehensible fate is, at best, nothing but the result of all our previous actions, their *vis inertiae*, the momentum they acquired when entering the physical and social course of the world. This fundamental homogeneity between previous actions, which were supposed to be free, and present fate, which is apparently suffered, is at the basis of an efficient medical action while at the same time, limiting its power. For, indeed, the total sum of energy born from a certain amount of past actions and flowing into a definitive present disease may exceed the one the doctor and his patient may have at their disposal. Hence we may use as a clue the notion of "immanent justice," provided we do not laicize or Westernize the position of Āyurveda to extremes. To this end, it is necessary to recall:

1. that his practitioners don't draw any clear-cut border line between lack of hygiene and moral offence — between external and internal purity; and
2. that they do not, even for a moment, think of limiting the past of an individual to the time elapsed since his — last — rebirth.

Origin and Curability of Diseases

Torn between two contradictories, at least for us, demands: the need to account for diseases and their prognosis in purely religious terms and the need to assign them a purely biological aetiology, Āyurvedic doctors opted for a certain form of compromise. They actually sort out ordinary frequent diseases whose kārmic part, though not quite disclaimed, is tacitly disregarded, from rare diseases with a mysterious aetiology — (taking into account the level of scientific knowledge of those times) — commonly understood as being the pure result of *karman*. The first ones are considered as curable and their detection and treatment constitute the bulk of therapeutic practice, the doctor's "daily bread." As to the other ones — specially leprosy (*kuṣṭha*) and tuberculosis (*yakṣman*) since they are considered as the punishment for particularly serious crimes such as murdering a brāhmaṇa or stealing his gold — committed in some previous life. As such, they are thought to be incurable to such an extent that, the doctor can resort only to a palliative treatment. Though they cannot be cured, these diseases do not call for a fatal prognosis. For, sometimes, we may come across a remission; even a spontaneous, total or partial, recovery may be seen. Such cases, readily mentioned in Āyurvedic literature, are, in no way, considered as exceptions to the rule of *karman*, even less as its contradiction. It is simply thought that such diseases can stop following their course, even decline, if the amount of suffering they have already caused counterbalances the seriousness of the sins the punishment of which they constitute.

Mental Diseases and "Lack of Wisdom"

Between ordinary diseases and kārmically loaded incurable diseases, Āyurveda ranks mental diseases in a category of their own. Theirs is a specially interesting case since it enables us to understand how the medical thought of ancient India paradoxically succeeds in making use of the very notion of *karman* to withdraw, partly at least, this sort of disease from the religious or sacred domain. Traditionally, indeed, for instance in Āyurveda — mental diseases and, more particularly, their symptoms: delirium, hallucinations, aggressive or phobic behaviour, prostration, etc. were understood in terms of "attacks," possession, by several categories of demons — *yakṣa, rākṣasa, vetāla*, etc. — or even "ghosts" dissatisfied for not having been honoured with the funeral rites their descendents should have practised for them. Facing such cases, medical thought unfolds into several stages. It suggests first — but does not assert — that these demons are but agents, means of "bearing fruit," for some aspects of the personal negative *karman* in a tortured individual. It then insinuates that these beings are not real but the product of fantasy, that is to say they stand for some mental projections within a psyche — cf. the notion of "subtle body" — tainted by previous impious deeds. They would embody the "sense of guilt" of the person in question, the remorse that keeps haunting him — in the double meaning of the term — in the guise of a voice or of various threatening visions. This is especially clear in the case of *preta*. Thirdly, these impious deeds are said to proceed from a general attitude "lacking in wisdom" — *prajñā-aparādha*. That is a notion not quite easy to understand, for its global meaning extends from mere lack of prudence — for instance in matters of food, heat or cold — to any sort of hybrids : exalted pride or thoughtless provocation, vain glory of a subject pertly behaving towards the upper Powers — gods, ancestors, *ṛṣis*, etc. Fourthly and lastly, on the basis of such reasoning, the properly religious notion of sins committed in a previous life no longer considerably differs from the secular, nearly rational notion of foolish behaviour we come across so frequently in this our life. So, there is a certain continuity between the aetiology of diseases thought to be organic — for instance, those due to overeating — and that of psychic diseases due, for instance to recklessly visiting at night such places of evil fame as crossroads, cremation places, etc. It then ensues that, despite differences in symptoms, the parallelism in causes may lead to a unified conception of disorders. In other words, the doctor may, in the last resort, equate ordinary, psychic as well as organic diseases with what Āyurveda considers as the very essence of morbidity, that is a certain lack of balance, due to some "lack of wisdom," between the fundamental components of the organism — *dhātu-vaiṣamya*; he can, then, fight this lack of balance as such.

The Problem of Heredity

Another particularly interesting case where naturalistic and "kārmic" explanations interfere is the question of heredity. The laws of genetics being totally ignored, the cases when the physical and psychological constitution of a new-born dramatically differs from that of its parents are a real problem. For instance, the child has a clear complexion whereas his father and mother are dark-skinned or it is, for its age, quick and sharp, whereas his parents are dull-witted, etc. Here too, the main tendency is, as much as possible, to limit the use of kārmic or religious explanatory structures. In short, all the physical and psychical particularities of the child that are still in keeping with the norm will be accounted for in terms of the circumstances in which it was conceived, of the respective tempers of the father and mother interfering with each other or, even, of the condition of living of the mother during pregnancy — diet, surroundings, etc. Conversely, all the exceptions to hereditary transmission bordering on monstruous or extraordinary cases are accounted for in exclusively kārmic terms. In this category are found defects, anomalies, congenital malformations — and this is similar to the view of such diseases as leprosy or tuberculosis — as well as the cases of children exceptionally precocious in walking, or talking, in which cases Āyurveda confesses its inability to specify the aetiology and keeps them purposely out of its field of action.

The Special Case of Epidemics

Natural catastrophes: floods, forest fires, earthquakes, etc. — not to forget wars — present a particular problem to the theory of *karman*, as they end with the almost simultaneous destruction of a large number of individual lives. For, on the one hand, according to the classical Indian way of thinking these unhappy events cannot but be the result of kārmic retribution. On the other hand, a fundamental rule of the theory of *karman* has it that "as you sow so you shall reap and no more" with the corollary "there is no payment — good or bad — for actions committed by others." Now, in the case of natural catastrophes in which thousands of people may die together, the rule of strictly individual kārmic retribution presents a difficult problem : how can the maturing process of actions — in this case probably more or less ancient deeds — running parallel within thousands of independent individual series suddenly converge to one, and the same, tragic end ? Now, with epidemics, which are more or less within their scope, doctors also meet with this problem.

Here too, they must keep to the principle of a kārmic origin of epidemics while taking into account the regularly attested presence of such original causes in stricken areas as faeces for cholera or marshes for malaria. In front of the situation, medical treatises — particularly that of Caraka — follow a regressive method. From noted symptoms, their description, their distribution among the population and their geographical localization, they first try to identify the polluting elements present in the surroundings — air, water, earth — of the affected groups. So doing, they pay a particular attention to the recently and specially obvious elements. Their way of proceeding, so far apparently "scientific," appears then to us somewhat disturbing. For it decidedly searches external nature for "bad omens," such signs in the sky as the apparition of comets, halos or eclipses, such meteorological signs as confusion of seasons, torrential or absent monsoons, etc. and such biological signs as the birth of animal or human monsters. To our eyes, these phenomena seem to make an incongruous medley; in their eyes, they share a common origin: all of them reveal that the universal order or *dharma* is out of joint. Let us recall that the notion of *dharma* includes the good working of society as well as the regular activity of external nature — the "socio-cosmic" order. Thus, from scattered evidence their "police inquiry" brings together converging signs — not noticed in time — of some disorder in the balance of nature.

They, then, have but to postulate that, when, in a given area, phenomena have not occurred according to a normal regularity, it means that the inhabitants of the area were, some time in the past, guilty of particularly serious offences to social morals and, so, have incurred, if not divine runition — as Sodom and Gomorrha in the Bible — at least receive the effect of the natural consequences of their acts. Let us yet remark that this particularly clever and subtle way to link kārmic causality with natural causality — the socio-cosmic disorder due to human action inducing a particular malignity of infectious germs endemically present in the surroundings — does not entirely solve the problem inherent to the individualized character of kārmic retribution, so that medical treatises continuously waver between two hypotheses. Either they assume that, in the past, a real collective sin was committed and produced a collective *karman*, or they fall back on the idea of innumerable separate individual *karman*s happening — nearly miraculously — to reach maturity together.

This being admitted, they have to resume their therapeutic approach and combine it with the properly religious *karman*. Practically there is a difference between, on the one hand, the direct "targets" of epidemics and their afore-known victims and, on the other, those not aimed at which are the mere prey of contagion. Of course, the two categories can be but a posteriori distinguished, from the lack of efficiency of treatments in the first case and from their successful effect in the second. Again, there is a striking parallel with the difference formerly noticed between "ordinary" diseases, curable because of possessing only a slight kārmic component, and "extraordinary" diseases, as incurable as leprosy and tuberculosis, of a basically kārmic origin. Nevertheless we should not overstress the distinction for, to some extent, the treatment applied to all patients — which works for some of them — always includes, besides proper medicinal elements — baths, massages, potions — such religious elements as fire offerings, the reciting of sacred phrases — *mantras* — etc. Now, in the treatises of *dharma* of the type "Laws of Manu," these religious practices are believed to be able preventively — before fruition — to render at least some small or medium types of negative *karman* harmless. And let us not forget a third way to solve the problem, a radical one because it cuts the Gordian knot rather than unties it. It consists in making only one person, to wit the king, responsible for the epidemics. This was relevant in ancient India where, to some extent, the king was actually considered as the owner of his kingdom and of its inhabitants. He, then, through his personal misdemeanour, could have called misfortune not only on himself but also on all his subjects. It was, then, his duty, both privately and publicly, to practise expiatory and propitiatory rites.

Conclusion

At the end of this too short review of medical literature what comes out is the ease with which Āyurveda is, on the one hand, careful never to run slap into the dogma of *karman*, the centre of the ethico-religious thought of India and, on the other hand, manages to prevent, as much as possible, this belief from interfering in positive medical reasoning, perverting the diagnosis and troubling the setting of the treatment. On that score, we cannot but see the parallel with what was noticed in the purely religious field. Both doctor and patient try to strip the *karman* from its opaque transcendent character, from its *"Deus ex machina"* status, to implant it a new into a living human activity whose objective or reified product, easily operated on, it would be.

But there still remains a paradox not touched upon by this literature. To wit: though certain ills, diseases and disabilities seem more or less avoidable or curable by medicine, they still retain their kārmic origin. The moral sins which would have been paid for by such and such disease, if it had not been treated, will have to be paid for with other ills, for instance mournings, disappointments, etc. One may wonder at the interest of a therapeutic practice which merely displaces suffering. There is a solution not considered in India — may be because the question has never really cropped up there — which solution was elsewhere outlined — see the notion of so-"compossibility" in ancient stoicism. It would, no doubt, mean postulating something like a divine omniscience, that would include in advance, while granting everyone the goods and ills due to his actions, *also* the results of the experiments, and successes, of doctors and other "technicians of a better living." Instead of that, according to late commentaries to classical medical treatises, Āyurveda tended more and more to invoke *karman* as a convenient explanation to all diseases and as a pretext to excuse humans from imagining new ways to fight them.

8

Classical Indian Philosophy in the Perspective of Cultural Studies
Sketching a New Approach

Victoria Lysenko

SINCE Indian philosophy become a subject of study in the West as well as in India there is no end to the controversy whether it is a genuine philosophy. Actually, this dispute takes for granted the existence of a certain general normative concept of philosophy, of which the different philosophical traditions are sub-varieties. Thus, in order to say what the content of Indian philosophy is, we have to come to agreement as to what we understand by philosophy as such. There are as many definitions of philosophy as there are philosophies or even philosophers. For example, "Philosophy is a theoretical inquiry into the fundamental questions of being," or "Philosophy is a kind of critical reasoning," or whatever it may be . . . the content of this general concept is established a priori and arbitrarily enough — it is either borrowed from the European tradition, from any well-known definition of philosophy (for instance, by Aristotle, Descartes, Hegel), or it is constructed on the basis of premises derived from the European philosophy. It is the most widespread approach to our problem of defining what Indian philosophy is.

At the same time, there is another approach which tries not to resort to such kind of definition (in logic we call it "intensive definitions"). Briefly speaking, according to this approach, national or regional philosophies proceed not from some generic essence of philosophy but from the cultural traditions, in which they arose. Each culture creates or does not create its philosophy. In the first case, a regional philosophy may include some elements that in other cultures remain external to the philosophical tradition proper to them. What was considered philosophy in Greece does not necessarily coincide with the idea of philosophy in India or in China. But at the same time it does not exclude a number of concurrent features, which can be interpreted as typologically common.

If the first approach is based on the genus-species relationship, the second reminds the logical notion of family likeness (*A* is like *B*, *B* is like *C*, therefore *A* is like *C* even if they have no common element). One can ask the question as to whether the researcher is capable of describing Indian philosophy without referring to his (or her) own culturally determined representation of what philosophy in general stands for. As shown by the history of the encounter between Western thinkers and India, "philosophy in general," or philosophy as a generic concept, is tacitly identified with philosophy as understood in the West. The second type of approach, it seems to me, is more advantageous, because the term "philosophy" here loses its historically loaded meaning and becomes only a conditional verbal mark which, in the absence of more accurate terms, may be used at the present stage of our knowledge about non-European traditions and which — in the final analysis — can be replaced by the local terms. But I am arguing that when in Indian studies scholars use the terms *darśana* or *ānvīkṣikī* as local names for "philosophy," a rather strong imprint of the first approach remains, because they have in mind some sort of generic definition of philosophy. The "supporters" of *darśana* lay stress on the practical religious import of Indian thought (for example, Sarvapalli Radhakrishnan), whereas the adherents of *ānvīkṣikī* insist on its rationalistic and critical activity (for example, Bimal Krishna Matilal). The division between these images of Indian philosophy is connected — in a rather clear-cut manner — with the fact that they are tightly associated with this or that image of philosophy in general. The second approach provides the scholar with more freedom of investigation, demanding at the same time more responsibility. The researcher is no more constrained by stereotypes as regards what exactly he (or she) should be looking for.

I suppose that the general strategy in treating Indian thought should start from an elucidation of the status and nature of knowledge in Indian culture. For this purpose, it is necessary to proceed to a sort of structural reconstruction of some basic principles on which the cultural integrity of India rests. The organic and integral character of the Indian tradition does not require any special proof. Now a question arises about the bases of this integrity, about what ties together its diverse orientations — for example, extreme austerity and extreme sensuality, or the ideal of other-worldliness, and cultivation of a rigid hierarchical social structure. India is famous not only for its variety of hermits and *yogins*, but also for its *Kāmasūtra*, a treatise on the art of love, where all possible ways of receiving and giving sensual pleasure are systematized and described in detail. However, in India, asceticism and eroticism are not so much opposed. We may refer to Tantrism where the sexual act is considered both an ascetic and a religious practice. A hierarchical social structure and a parallel quasi-egalitarian community of ascetics not only do not contradict but necessarily supplement each other. In the absence of any opportunity to escape from the closed space of the caste system, the latter by itself would have been socially explosive and would not have lasted for so many centuries.

All these "contrasts" taken together, while giving all-encompassing account of all logical modlities of a specialized human activity, hare in common a cult of skill, or in more philosophical parlance, a hypostization of function. Indian society is made up not of individuals, or citizens, but of personifications of the professional functions. However, this phenomenon proceeds from a certain Indian attitude towards the cosmos, society, culture and the position of man in it. The latter from my point of view, was based, in its turn on a strict distribution of functions between the various elements of the Hindu socio-cosmic hierarchical system.

Traditional Hindu culture presents itself as a hierarchy of four systems of concepts: four *varṇa*s or social categories (brāhmaṇa, kṣatriya, vaiśya and śūdra), four stages of life (*āśrama*: *brahmacarya, gṛhastha, vānaprastha* and *saṁnyāsa*), four aims of life (*puruṣārtha — dharma, artha, kāma* and *mokṣa*) and three ways to the realization of the religious goal — the *mokṣa* (*karma-mārga, jñāna-mārga*, and *bhakti-mārga*). The *varṇa* system is built on a kind of "division of labour", or division of functions among different *varṇa*s. This type of social construction appears to be a functional whole that receives its identity from each of its elements carrying out its own function (by contrast with another type of whole which call "an additional" because it is considered as a summation of its parts).

We may notice that in each of the systems listed above there is a certain asymmetry. The fourth and the highest step of a hierarchical ladder appears already to be lying outside the hierarchy as such. Among the *varṇa*s it is the brāhmaṇa, among *āśrama*s — the *saṁnyāsa*, among *puruṣārtha*s — the *mokṣa* and among ways to emancipation — the *jñāna-mārga*. All of them are described in Indian tradition as *nivṛtti*, literally non-functioning, in contrast to *pravṛtti*, or functioning, which covers the first three steps (two for *mārga*s). *Pravṛtti* is a general designation of any sort of activity, including the action of the *karman* — moral retribution in the circle of *saṁsāra*. *Nivṛtti*, the cessation of activity, associated with pure contemplation, can be also understood as a disinterested action or inactivity in activity, which does not leave any karmic traces, susceptible of promoting the further reincarnation of the individual.

It may seem that the last step of the hierarchy eliminates any value in the hierarchy as such. Actually, the hierarchy is there only to be rejected, as the scaffoldings are dismantled once the house is ready. In fact, the hierarchical character is relevant only to the sphere of *pravṛtti* — mundane activity. It is within this sphere that Indians favour the idea of order and distribution of functions, — that is the idea of *dharma*. In the sphere of *nivṛtti* there cannot be any hierarchy or order, as it does not involve any distinction of degrees — it is impossible to be half or three-quarter emancipated, in the same way as it is impossible for a woman to be half pregnant.

This hierarchical picture is too structured and systematic to have arisen purely spontaneously. No doubt, it developed out of some fundamental principles and values that are to be looked for in the early stages of Indian history. It seems to me that the roots of such a construction of the Hindu socio-cosmological order lay in the ritualistic system developed in classical Brāhmanism (in texts like Brāhmaṇas, Āraṇyakas and Upaniṣads). The Brāhmanic ritualism is unique in the sense that the sacrifice it describes appears to be a centre of religious and social life, around which all the rest revolves. The main contribution of ritual to the generation of the cultural paradigm is a precise division of functions between its participants, their hierarchical arrangement and an extreme attention to formal aspects of action, as it was considered that rituals sustain the cosmic order, so that even the smallest formal error could result in a universal catastrophe. From this are derived the major culture-generating principles: functionality, hierarchical character and system integrity supported by the accurate execution by each agent of its own function (what I call here a principle of functional whole).

Four principal categories of priests took part in sacrifices. For example, in the *soma* ritual cantors supervised by the *Udgātṛ* periodically execute "tunes" (*sāman*). Every tune is accompanied by a loud recitation of hymns (*ṛc*) interpreted by the *Hotṛ*. At the same time, another priest, the Adhvaryu, performs certain actions like pouring oil into the fire while uttering in a low voice special formulas (*yajus*). There is a fourth priest, the brāhmaṇa, whose sole task consists in surveying the whole process and reproducing it mentally to ensure that not the slightest fault is committed. In the ritual system, the brahmin is a key figure in the sense that he encompasses in his mind the totality of ritual procedures and for this reason may be regarded as a bearer of its wholeness and completeness. What he is responsible for pertains not to this or that ritual function however important it may be, but to the general import of the ritual ceremony in its entirety. We may ask why? The answer will be as follows: the brāhmaṇa possesses the most secret formula containing the essence of the ritual, which is referred to as *brahman*. In case of any infringement of ritual procedure, he is supposed to interfere and to correct the mistake, otherwise he stands outside the ritual, estranged from concrete actions (there is a remarkable resemblance of his role and the future doctrine of *sākṣin*, or the witness, in some systems of Indian philosophy). Symptomatically enough, also in the *varṇa* system, he is both inside and outside. His transcending the hierarchical principle is symbolized by his special relation to *saṁnyāsa* and *mokṣa* (though the members of other high *varṇas*, kṣatriyas and vaiśyas, have access to them, brāhmaṇa, being at the top of hieharchical system, is somehow more closely associated with these highest levels of other hierarchical orders). On the other side, his engagement in a hierarchical order is provided for by his being a part of the *varṇa-āśrama* system and by his sharing the values (*puruṣārtha*) incorporated in the category of *pravṛtti*.

From this we can see that the status of brāhmaṇa is far from being clear-cut. As was shown by the well-known indologist Jan Heesterman, the brāhmaṇa's status is a source of an important inner conflict in the Indian tradition (Jan Heesterman, *The Inner Conflict of Tradition*, Chicago: Chicago University Press, 1985). This conflict characterizes the sphere of relations between an ideal of the anchorite, embodied in the figure of brāhmaṇa, and a real social life embodied in the figure of kṣatriya, or secular governor. Actually, the conflict is between two kinds of authority — the secular one and the spiritual one: to make his power authoritative, the kṣatriya should receive an anointment from the brāhmaṇa. On the other side, the latter should not interfere in mundane affairs, though the material support of the kṣatriya and society is indispensable to him. Thus, the status of brāhmaṇa is quite ambivalent: his authority is based on the non-attachment to mundane affairs nevertheless, his very existence directly depends on society cultivating such an ideal.

That means that alongside the functionality of the hierarchical system there is something else that provides its integrity. If the members of the system are just "cogs in a machine," the brāhmaṇa acts as the carrier of integrity. What entitles him to play that role? — The possession of the higher knowledge of reality that is acquired in an extra-rational manner — the knowledge which is identical to the essence of being. It is designated by different terms — *vidyā, jñāna, prajñā, pratibhā,* etc. This knowledge is the common source of all the Śāstras, concrete knowledge in the different spheres of activity. According to tradition, all the Śāstras proceed from the gods or sacred seers — *ṛṣi,* handed down from generation to generation through an uninterrupted chain of teachers and pupils.

The Indian tradition — and this makes its uniqueness — believes that the higher knowledge (contained first of all in the Vedas or other sacred texts) pre-exists the development of human history. Such primordial and a priori knowledge is the most complete and exhaustive. However, taking into account the limited capacities of man and the brevity of his life, the gods and the seers have adapted it to human level, gradually reducing and simplifying its contents. Thus, it reaches the mankind in a considerably truncated form. It is supposed that the closer the Śāstra lies to its pre-historic original source, the more authoritative and authentic it is. Nobody is capable of producing any new idea or doctrine, that wasn't already contained in this primordial knowledge and, consequently, the development of Śāstra should be viewed not in a perspective of accumulating new knowledge in the future, but in a sort of retrospection — returning back to its initial completeness in the past. The true knowledge is a prerogative of the past, not of the future. The idea of a progress in the field of knowledge was univocally reduced to the idea of a regress — an eternal returning to sources.

The traditional method of learning Śāstra follows the model provided by the study of the Veda. It is not a simple training but an initiation into a certain special state of knowledge. At the first stage, the pupil repeats the Vedic formulas after his teacher in a purely mechanical manner. When he has memorized them, the teacher introduces him to the commentaries and gives his own explanations. At this stage, the pupil begins to understand all that he has memorized thoughtlessly before, and gradually or quite suddenly there arises in him a feeling of the wholeness and the unity of Vedic knowledge and he identifies himself with it. With this enlightenment the training comes to its culmination and the pupil himself becomes a teacher. Actually, the whole process may be viewed as a reproduction in him of the person of his teacher, or to put it differently, a reconstitution of a primary state of being permeated by the knowledge proper both to gods and ancient seers (*ṛṣi*).

Philosophical knowledge is a Śāstra in its own right. All religio-philosophical systems of Hinduism (except for the most "orthodox" of them — the Mīmāṁsā) proclaim as their supreme goal the attaining of *mokṣa*. Thus, philosophical wisdom correlates with the fourth and highest level of all hierarchical orders — the status of the brāhmaṇa, the *saṁnyāsin*, the *mokṣa* and the way of knowledge (*jñāna-mārga*). In other words, philosophical knowledge ideally refers to the sphere of *nivṛtti*. However, does this hold true in the actual practice of traditional Hindu culture?

It seems to me that the dual role of the brāhmaṇa, who is the main traditional bearer of philosophical knowledge, towards the society, results in a dual attitude of philosophy towards the cultural and social sphere. On the one hand, the philosophy, as well as the brāhmaṇa, should stay aloof from world affairs, cultural and social processes. It should deliver knowledge capable of releasing man from infinite rebirths. However, this knowledge involves an understanding and explanation of the structure of the world and the place and the role of man. Moreover, the society perceives philosophy not only as one of the possible ways to salvation but also as the quintessence of learning, instruction and scholarship, which it aspires to acquire and from which it wants to receive methods applicable to more worldly tasks.

As a means of attaining *mokṣa* all philosophical systems are rendered in Hinduism as *ātmavidyā* (and later also as *darśana*). As a method of understanding and explaining the world they are rendered as *anvīkṣikī, tarka, yukti* — all these terms designate logical methods of reasoning and analysis, which can be applied in different spheres. However, the analytical rational knowledge in the form transmitted from teacher to pupil, has never acquired a fully independent theoretical character and remained connected with religious salvation. An instrument as such is something relative — it can be more or less convenient or more or less efficient. Thus, it always depends on a set of different factors — on its user and on what it is being used for (*mokṣa* or mundane goals). Taking into account the traditional subservience of the Indian philosophical tradition (Śāstra) to the ideal of *mokṣa* (we do not discuss here the question as to what extent this subservience was always the case), we can explain the fact that in Indian culture, philosophy and religion were never separated from and opposed to each other, as well as the fact that philosophical knowledge was supposed to carry a practical (soteriological) character.

Once the higher knowledge is attained there is no more intellectual activity whatsoever (*nivṛtti*). However, the specificity of the philosophical Śāstra consists in requiring the way to such a higher knowledge to pass through knowledge understood as thinking, intellectual activity (*pravṛtti*) consisting in the manipulation with concepts according to logical laws that structure and organize its proceeding. This rational knowledge — in order to be efficient — should be correctly adjusted, or in Indian terms, it should be a *pramā* — "right measure," true knowledge "commensurable" to the instruments of its reception — the *pramāṇas*, of which the main ones were perception and logical inference. This latter aspect of philosophical activity corresponds to the cultural paradigm which we have characterized as commited to the functionality.

All Indian philosophical systems included, Buddhism and Jainism on the one hand, contain a component of a higher knowledge (verbalized as in the Nyāya and the Vaiśeṣika, or not verbalized as, for instance, in the Vedānta and Buddhism). On the other hand, they provide some kind of intellectual, rational interpretation of the world around us.

Thus, philosophy as a Śāstra — and this makes it unique among Śāstras — combines in itself two major structure-generating paradigms of Indian culture — the principle of super-hierarchical socio-cosmic integrity (cp. *ātmavidyā*) and the principle of hierarchical functionality (cp. *anvīkṣikī*). This approach (which in the present communication was but just sketched out) may help us to avoid a reduction of the Indian phenomenon of philosophy to some artificially constructed idea and, in that way, to avoid an isolation of Indian philosophy from its own cultural and historical context.

See My Other Contributions to the Same Topic

"Darśana, Anvīkṣikī and Dharma, Philosophy and Religion in India," in *Methodological Problems in Studies of History of Foreign Philosophy*, Moscow: Oriental Literature Publishing House, 1987, pp. 94-116 (in Russian).

"Comparative Philosophy in the Soviet Union," in *Philosophy East and West, A Quarterly of Comparative Philosophy*, Honolulu, vol. 42, Number 2, 1992, pp. 309-26.

"On Certain Intellectual Stereotypes as Exemplified in Th. Stcherbatsky's works," in *Journal of Indian Council of Philosophical Research*, Delhi, 1992, vol. 9, N 2, pp. 87-93.

"Classical Indian Philosophy in Studies and Translations of Russian Scholars (1990-1996)," *Problems of the Modern Historiography of the Philosophy of the Foreign Orient*, Moscow, Institute of Philosophy, 1998 (in Russian).

Padārtha-dharma-saṁgraha of Praśastapāda with Nyāyakandalī of *Śrīdhara*, Translation from Sanskrit into Russian, Introduction, Historico-philosophical commentary, Notes and Indices by Victoria Lysenko . Moscow, Vostochnaya Literatura, 2005 (in Russian) 760 p.

Index